SUPERSTARS OF THE
PREMIER
LEAGUE

SUPERSTARS OF THE
PREMIER
LEAGUE

Jim Drewett & Alex Leith

P

||| • PARRAGON • |||

**First published in Great Britain in 1998 by
Parragon
13 Whiteladies Road
Clifton
Bristol BS8 1PB**

Copyright © 1998 Parragon

ISBN: 0-75252-561-1

**Produced for Parragon
by Prima Creative Services**

**Editorial director Roger Kean
Project editor Oliver Frey**

Design and repro by Prima Creative Services

Printed and bound in Italy

Acknowledgements
The Mitre® football and logo are used courtesy of
Pentland Sports Group – many thanks to
Sarah Reynolds.

Background illustration by Oliver Frey

Picture Acknowledgements
The publisher would like to thank Allsport for their help and the kind permission to reproduce the photographs used in this book.
Allsport Photographers:
Shaun Botterill; 6, 8, 32, 35, 62, 71, 78, 85, 86
Clive Brunskill; 28, 30, 41, 42, 43, 48, 55, 57, 58
David Cannon; 92
Graham Chadwick; 50
Phil Cole; 9, 15, 23, 28, 36, 37, 51, 56, 69, 88, 96
Stu Forster 7, 64, 65, 66, 72, 73, 76, 77, 80, 81, 82, 83
Laurence Griffiths; 29, 74
Mike Hewitt; 11, 13, 47
Ross Kinnaird; 11, 31, 38, 39, 40, 44, 52, 67, 79
Alex Livesey; 16, 75, 93, 94
Craig Prentis; 27
Gary M Prior; 14, 49, 84
Ben Radford; 33, 34, 59, 61, 63, 89
Dan Smith; 45
Mark Thompson; 17, 22, 53, 68, 70

Born to win

ight now the Carling Premiership is the most exciting league in the world. Great clubs, magnificent stadiums, huge crowds and some of the best managers in the world. But all these things would mean nothing without the 11 men who pull on their club colours and do the business on the pitch every week. Men who, with a flick of a boot or a drop of the shoulder, have the ability to leave 50,000 people all holding their breath at once... or have those same 50,000 people as one leaping out of their seats in unbridled joy. These men are truly the Superstars of the Premier League, and over the next 91 pages you can get a bit closer to discovering exactly what makes them tick... well, 42 of the very best of them, anyway.

From Tony Adams to Gianfranco Zola, the cream of Europe's – and indeed the world's – footballers are more and more finding themselves attracted to the Premiership. It's on the playing fields of England that men like Dennis Bergkamp and Roberto Di Matteo are coming to test their skills against the very best. Meanwhile as our clubs strive harder and harder to get to – or keep – their place at the very top, home-grown stars like the electric Michael Owen and Manchester United's David Beckham are proving that the production line for producing world class talent hasn't dried up over here either.

This book is dedicated to players like these. Players who are blessed with skills and talent that most of us can only dream of. Players whose breathtaking ability to perform miracles with a ball make ours the best league in the world. Players who have rightly earned the title "Superstars of the Premier League".

Tony Adams

ARSENAL

> "My philosophy now is that I do the best I possibly can for me, and by doing the best for me I'm helping everybody else."

Age:
32

Date of birth
10.10.66

Birthplace
London

Nickname
None

Position
Defender

Games & Goals
Arsenal 421 (30)

Transfers
None. Signed professional forms from trainee in January 1984.

Honours
(all with Arsenal)
Division One champions 1989 and 1991
Premiership champions 1998
FA Cup 1993, 1998
Football League Cup 1987 and 1993
European Cup Winners' Cup 1994
Premier League, FA Cup 1998

THIS PAGE: CAPTAINING ARSENAL TO GLORY, AGAINST ALL PERSONAL ODDS

OPPOSITE PAGE: ADAMS RISES HIGH – AND SCORES AGAINST WIMBLEDON, 12 APRIL, 1998

f Tony Adams had put his hand up at school as often as he does in the Arsenal back four he might now be a brain surgeon. Medicine's loss, though, was football's gain as the Gunners captain is now widely recognized as one of the best defenders in the country as well as being a Highbury living legend.

Adams has had his problems in the past few years – notably a well-publicized battle with alcoholism and severe ankle, knee and back injuries – but has always fought back, making more returns to first-team action than Cindy Beale has to Albert Square. Despite missing a sizeable chunk of last season through injury, Adams still made a vital contribution to the Gunners' spectacular run of post-Christmas results which gave them their shot at the Double.

Little wonder, then, that Arsenal manager Arsene Wenger pays this glowing tribute to his captain: "He and his determination are respected by everybody," says the Frenchman. "He is a big influence here at the club, a good individual player, tactically strong and someone who reads the game well and quickly."

According to Wenger, Adams already shows many of the qualities of a manager-in-the-making. "Because he is very sensitive he feels what's happening in the dressing-room. He knows where the problems lie among the players, and between them they all get solved."

Few would doubt that Adams possesses sufficient credentials to make a bigger impression than most on the managerial merry-go-round. For now, though, he is concentrating only on extracting maximum benefit from the remainder of a playing career which has seen him collect enough silverware to open a branch of Ratner's. "You get the realization that you're not going to have it for ever and that one day the legs will stop running," he says. "So I'm trying to grasp the moment in games and keep on playing and enjoying it as long as I can. It has been a rejuvenation for me."

Premiership strikers be warned – it seems they can expect to see Tony Adams pointing his arm towards the heavens for a good few more years yet.

David Batty

NEWCASTLE UNITED

"There is only one way to prove you are the best team, and that's by winning the league. It's as simple as that."

Age
29

Date of Birth
2.12.68

Birthplace
Leeds

Nickname
None

Position
Midfielder

Games & Goals
Leeds United 211 (4),
Blackburn Rovers 54 (1)
Newcastle United 75 (3)

Transfers
October 1993 – Leeds United to
Blackburn Rovers (£2,75m)
March 1996 – Blackburn Rovers to
Newcastle United (£3,75m)

Honours
Division One title 1992
Division Two title 1990

THIS PAGE: UNASSUMING, BUT DEFINITELY ON THE BALL

OPPOSITE PAGE: BATTY'S PASSES FIND THEIR MARK NINE TIMES OUT OF TEN

The ball hits an Aston Villa defender and spins out to the Newcastle number four just outside the box. The way it drops invites a volley, and indeed the midfielder hits the ball before it lands on the ground. You know it's gone in before it fizzes, spinning, past Mark Bosnich's outstretched arm and into the net. A goal, three vital points in the bag and another corker from David Batty. He doesn't score them very often but when he does he makes sure they're a contender for Goal of the Month.

Not many Newcastle (or England) fans mind Batty's goal-shyness. He does, after all, do everything else required of a midfielder, and does it in bucketfuls. The blond short-haired player hardly puts a pass wrong, and rarely is there anyone on the pitch who makes as many passes. Keeping possession is Batty's religion and, even when under intense pressure from the opposition, nine out of ten times there's a Newcastle player at the end of one of his passes.

Keeping possession is one thing: gaining it is quite another, and it is another of the midfielder's fortes. No opponent looks forward to playing against Batty, so ferocious is his tackling. It means, of course, that he's no stranger to the referee's book, though seeing red at Chelsea in 1996/97 was the first time he was forced to go for an early bath in a career that stretches back to 1987.

The only reason the quiet, unassuming Leeds-born youth stopped watching his local team from the Elland Road Kop that year was that they signed him up to play for them and put him out on the pitch instead. He helped his team to the Championship in 1992, and, having been signed up by Blackburn in 1993 was in the team that clinched the Championship there three years later – though as he'd been out with an injury much of the season he refused the medal that was offered him.

Denied a different-club hat-trick of titles with Newcastle as the Magpies just missed out on the title under Keegan, who signed him for £3.75m in 1996, he is one of the few who has survived the Dalglish takeover and has changed from being an unpopular choice amongst neutral fans in the England team to one of its cornerstones. He's Nobby Stiles, in effect, with knobs on.

David Beckham

MANCHESTER UNITED

> "I always said that once I met Victoria I would be with her. She's my idea of perfection."

Age
23

Date of Birth
2.5.75

Birthplace
Leytonstone

Nickname
Becks

Position
Midfielder

Games & Goals
Manchester United 110 (23)
Preston North End (loan) 5 (2)

Transfers
None

Honours
Premiership 1996, 1997
FA Cup 1996

THIS PAGE: IN ACTION AGAINST ARSENAL, 14 MARCH, 1998

OPPOSITE PAGE: ADDING SPICE AND GENIUS TO MANCHESTER UNITED

David Beckham curls the ball around the Chelsea wall, beyond the reach of goalkeeper Ed de Goey and into the back of the net. He races towards the jubilant Manchester United fans, slides to the ground and cups his hands to his ears.

It may not have been the wackiest goal celebration of the season, but Beckham's post-goal routine in an FA Cup tie at Stamford Bridge carried a clear message to the home supporters: "You're not mocking my chick now!"

Lots of footballers have to put up with abuse about their expanding waistlines or receding hairlines, but David Beckham is unique in having to contend with spiteful taunts about his relationship with his girlfriend.

Then again, most players would readily accept the occasional dirty ditty from foul-mouthed fans if they could swap places with Beckham and snuggle up every evening with Victoria Adams, aka Posh Spice.

And it's not only Beckham's bird they'd like to have – they'd also love to possess his skill on the pitch, or at least a small fraction of it. Genius is an overused word in the world of football, but in Beckham's case it is not merely hyperbole.

Put simply, the London-born star has all the attributes of the complete midfield player: he can unlock a defence with a killer pass, leave defenders standing with a sway of his snake-like hips, win tackles against the toughest of opponents and... oh, he can shoot from just about anywhere (just ask Wimbledon keeper Neil Sullivan!).

Rumour has it that Beckham may soon be on his way to a top Italian club, but whatever the future holds, he is certain to be a key figure in England's bid for European championship glory. Manchester United legend George Best even suggests Glenn Hoddle should make the floppy-haired youngster his skipper. "Give him the captaincy," he urges, "give him the centre of midfield, give him the authority, give him whatever it takes. I think so highly of Beckham that he could become the Eric Cantona of Manchester United and he could reach similar heights for England." Some reference; some player.

Dennis Bergkamp
ARSENAL

> "I've always believed that when you practise a lot with the ball you reach a stage where you can do everything you want."

Age
29

Date of Birth
18.5.69

Birthplace
Amsterdam

Nickname
The Iceman

Position
Striker

Games & Goals
Ajax 185 (103), Inter Milan 52 (11)
Arsenal 90 (38)

Transfers
July 1993 – Ajax to Inter Milan (£8m)
July 1995 – Inter Milan to Arsenal (£7,5m)

Honours
Dutch Championship 1990
Dutch Cup 1987, 1993
European Cup Winners' Cup 1987
UEFA Cup 1992 (Ajax), 1994 (Inter)
Premier League, FA Cup 1998

THIS PAGE: EFFORTLESS BRILLIANCE AGAINST LEEDS

OPPOSITE PAGE: BERGKAMP'S AUDACIOUS PLAY WAS SADLY MISSED AT ARSENAL'S DOUBLE-WIN WEMBLEY FA CUP FINAL

Last season Dennis Bergkamp picked up enough silverware to set up a store in Hatton Garden, the centre of London's precious metal trade. First up, he walked off with the PFA's Footballer of the Year award; then he picked up an FA Cup winner's medal with Arsenal; don't forget, too, that he made a habit of winning Match of the Day's Goal of the Month competition, including an amazing clean sweep of the first three places in August.

Those three goals – a mazy dribble and dead-eyed shot against Southampton, a beautifully flighted curler against Leicester and an audacious piece of ball-juggling and cool finish in the same match – were merely some of the highlights of Bergkamp's explosive start to the season.

It couldn't last and it didn't. Not because he lost anything of his effortless brilliance (if his form dipped a little it was still at a level other players could only dream about). No, the problem was with his temperament. Suddenly, the man who used to make a snowman look hot-blooded was finding himself wound up by the rough stuff handed out by the Premiership's bully boys.

Two suspensions followed, and the Dutchman missed some of the most vital games of Arsenal's Double-chasing season. Without him The Gunners still managed to chalk up a few of their customary 1–0 victories, but their play lacked beauty, elegance and sparkle.

Arsenal boss Arsene Wenger is the first to appreciate what Bergkamp brings to the side. "He is always the best, he is vital," says Wenger. "He improves the confidence of the whole team. When he plays well, everyone else does. He is certainly world-class and if you ask me if he is the best player in the Premiership, I can say that he definitely is in that position."

World class, but not world traveller. Bergkamp famously hates flying (even a TV advert for British Airways brings him out in a cold sweat) and, like last season, will stay at home if Arsenal's European campaign demands a trip to the outer reaches of the continent. Arsenal fans will be praying the draw gives them opposition within easy reach of the Channel Tunnel.

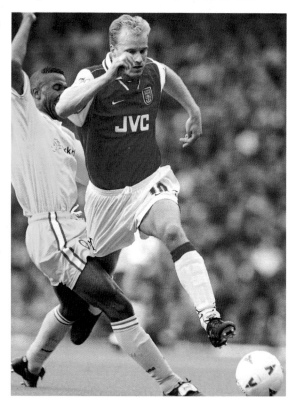

Eyal Berkovic

WEST HAM UNITED

"Life in England is very quiet compared to Israel, where because of the political and economical situation things can be very tense."

Age
26

Date of Birth
2.4.72

Birthplace
Haifa, Israel

Nickname
Berko

Position
Midfielder

Games & Goals
Southampton 28 (4)
West Ham United 35 (7)

Transfers
October 1996 – Maccabi Tel Aviv to Southampton (lease)
July 1997 – Southampton to West Ham United (£1,5m)

Honours
None

THIS PAGE: AT THE HEART OF WEST HAM'S BEST ATTACKS

OPPOSITE PAGE: EYING A GOAL-SCORING CHANCE AGAINST ASTON VILLA ON 15 OCTOBER, 1997

Eyal Berkovic's first season for West Ham was so packed with incident and controversy it could have been scripted by a half-crazed soap opera writer. First, there was a much-publicized on-pitch bust-up with teammate John Moncur at Chelsea; then, the Israeli claimed he was racially abused by two Blackburn players following a clash with Kevin Gallagher which led to the Rovers striker being sent off; finally, the midfielder had to defend himself against allegations that he was "a diver".

Unfortunately, the headlines generated by these incidents tended to detract attention from Berkovic's superb contribution on the park as The Hammers surged towards a European place. With his ability to thread a defence-splitting ball through even the tightest of rearguards, allied to excellent close ball skills and an eye for a goalscoring chance, the Haifa-born playmaker was at the heart of most of West Ham's best attacking moves.

Berkovic's consistent performances meant he soon achieved cult status at Upton Park – the West Ham faithful no doubt immensely grateful that the former Southampton player had chosen to parade his talents in the East End rather than a few miles north at White Hart Lane.

When his contract ran out at The Dell, Berkovic had talks with Spurs and was under pressure from his family and friends to sign for the North Londoners. "Spurs are a Jewish club," he says. "The chairman and many of the supporters are Jewish, and that is why most people thought I would go there."

Berkovic can thank his agent for saving him from a dispiriting year with the Premiership strugglers. "He told me I could succeed better at West Ham, that they play technical football, and that they would play around me. That is what Harry Redknapp told me, too."

Redknapp wasn't fibbing, either, and gave Berkovic a free reign to run The Hammers' midfield. This season he will be looking to do the same as West Ham attempt to conquer Europe. Who knows, he may even find himself rooming with his old sparring partner, John Moncur, on away trips. "Now we are friends," enthuses Berkovic, "in fact, we are very good friends."

Sol Campbell

TOTTENHAM HOTSPUR

"I'm glad I come from East London because in many ways that's much harder than anything football can throw at you."

How do you explain the paradox that Sol Campbell – probably England's strongest and most versatile defender – plays his club football for a team with one of the Premiership's flimsiest defences? It's a bit like spotting TV chef Keith Floyd serving egg and chips in your local greasy spoon or Naomi Campbell modelling sweaters for a mail-order knitwear company.

Not that Campbell had much time for cooking (or knitting) last season – he was too busy attempting to plug the gaps in Tottenham's leaking backline. Nevertheless, even a player of his natural athleticism, power and strength was unable to prevent the Lillywhites from being on the wrong end of some embarrassing thrashings.

Despite Spurs' depressing form, Campbell's own performances rarely dipped below the high standard he has maintained since he marked his first team debut, aged 18, with a goal against Chelsea in December 1992. Throughout a difficult nine months at White Hart Lane Campbell remained focused on the job in hand – saving the North London giants from the humiliating prospect of League dates with the likes of Stockport, Bury and Oxford.

As captain of the side Campbell performed a vital role. He played at the back, but led from the front, setting a shining example for some of his under-achieving teammates. Even a disruptive change in manager and the running feud between Christian Gross and Jurgen Klinsmann failed to affect him. "Sometimes, y'know, you've got to go through the chaos to get to the calm," he says.

Calm – now there's a word that just about sums up Sol. After all, this is a man who walked into the bear-pit of Rome's Olympic Stadium and dealt with everything Italy threw at him during England's epic World Cup qualifier last October.

Campbell's spirited performance that night was especially pleasing for the tough-tackling centre-back as it erased the memory of his Wembley gaffe which allowed Gianfranco Zola to score the only goal in the first encounter between the two teams. In Rome, though, the home side might as well have fielded Emile Zola – the nineteenth century French author – as the tiny forward was completely marked out of the game by the Sol Man.

Age
23

Date of birth
18.9.74

Birthplace
Stratford

Nickname
Sol-Man

Position
Defender

Games & Goals
Tottenham Hotspur 168 (2)

Transfers
None. Signed pro forms from trainee in September 1992

Honours
None

THIS PAGE: SOL CAMPBELL DISPLAYS CALM STRENGTH AND ATHLETICISM

OPPOSITE PAGE: SOL-MAN RACES TO PLUG A DEFENSIVE HOLE

Andy Cole

MANCHESTER UNITED

"To play in this United team really makes me smile because I know we are considered a good side."

Andy Cole doesn't so much receive the ball as sprint onto it just inside Chelsea's half. He looks to be at full speed, but he's not. A quick change of acceleration and he's away from Leboeuf, and the Frenchman's no slouch. There seems to be only one option for him as he enters Chelsea's box, wide on the left: a cross on to Sheringham, who has somehow managed to keep up and get into the box. He's at far too narrow an angle for a shot. Or is he? The answer lies in the back of the net, behind a quizzical Ed de Goey who didn't know the ball could be hit so hard. Chelsea are out of the Cup and if Cole still has any detractors they're hiding in their bunkers.

Detractors, however, there were, especially after the London-born striker's well-publicized move from Newcastle to Manchester for £6.5 million and an Irish winger in 1994/95. He was almost immediately dubbed a flop, and, before last season, a waste of money, despite bagging 30 goals for the club in 70-odd appearances and helping United to consecutive championships. "He's lost it," they were saying; "he'll never be the same player again."

The truth was, United weren't playing to Cole's strengths. He was part of a Cantona-inspired attack that passed the ball about in the opposition half, patiently waiting for a hole in the opponents' defence to appear before thrusting in the rapier. He was becoming a better all-round player, but his strike ratio, which had always before been high, was suffering.

Cole, with a Greaves-like change of pace and a ferocious first-time shot is much more suited to the style of play United employed in 1997/98: quick attacks at pace, that out-run rather than outwit the defenders. He thrives on the ball he can run onto, as he demonstrated at Newcastle. On Tyneside he had Beardsley to look out for his runs and feed him the ball. At United there's Beckham, Sheringham, Giggs and Scholes: no wonder he's thriving. A hat-trick in the Champions League against Feyenoord in Rotterdam signalled Cole was back to his very best again. "Andy's showing what I bought him for, and that's fantastic," said his manager Alex Ferguson afterwards. And he meant goals, of course.

Age	
26	
Date of Birth	
15.10.71	
Birthplace	
Nottingham	
Nickname	
Coley	
Position	
Striker	

Goals & Games
Arsenal 1 (0), Fulham (loan) 13 (3)
Bristol City 41 (20)
Newcastle United 70 (55)
Manchester United 105 (45)

Transfers
July 1992 – Arsenal to Bristol City (£500,000)
February 1993 – Bristol City to Newcastle United (£1,75m)
January 1995 – Newcastle United to Manchester United (£7m)

Honours
Premiership 1996, 1997
Division One 1993, FA Cup 1996

THIS PAGE: HOLDING BOLTON AT BAY

OPPOSITE PAGE: THRIVING WITH MANCHESTER UNITED, 5 DECEMBER, 1997

Roberto Di Matteo

CHELSEA

"I just enjoy playing with Chelsea and living in London."

oberto Di Matteo had to admit that his mother wasn't too pleased when he shaved off all his hair last season. Signora Di Matteo probably had a point, too. With his permanently tanned skin and vaguely oriental features her son's entry into the crowded Stamford Bridge baldies' club left him looking uncannily like a young Bhuddist monk.

Chelsea fans, though, won't mind if Di Matteo dyes his hair pink – as long as he continues to smash in long-range howitzers like the one which ripped past Arsenal keeper Alex Manninger in the Coca-Cola Cup semi-final.

"It was another goal that nobody could expect," said Di Matteo afterwards. No prizes, by the way, for guessing that "the other goal" he was referring to was that 35-yard corker after just 43 seconds in the 1997 FA Cup Final against Middlesbrough.

Thunderbolts from outrageous distances have become a Di Matteo trademark. But there's a lot more to his game than the ability to make goalkeepers tremble every time he approaches the box. Slide rule passing, excellent ball skills and tough tackling make the Swiss-born Italian one of the most complete midfielders in Europe.

So well, in fact, that Di Matteo – a £4.9 million signing from Lazio in the summer of 1996 – is now an automatic choice for the Italian national team despite having to face competition from some of the finest players in Serie A for his midfield berth. While the likes of Roberto Baggio and Alessandro Del Piero fight over the best position on the bench, Di Matteo is just about the first name on Cesare Maldini's team sheet every game.

Perhaps his secret lies in his socks which, bizarrely, he chooses to wear over his knees. "It's just a habit," he explains, "it's not because I have to. It's because I played with them like this in Switzerland when we (FC Aarau) won the championship." Now the man with the longest socks in England is aiming for the Premiership title.

Age
27

Date of Birth
29.5.70

Birthplace
Schaffhausen, Switzerland

Nickname
Robbie

Position
Midfielder

Games & Goals	
Schaffhausen 50 (2)	Zurich 34 (6)
Aarau 32 (1)	Lazio 88 (7)
Chelsea 64 (11)	

Transfer
July 1996 - Lazio to Chelsea (£4,9)

Honours
Swiss Championship 1992/93 (FC Aarau)
FA Cup 1997
Coca-Cola Cup 1998
European Cup Winners' Cup 1998

THIS PAGE: AVOIDING ASTON VILLA'S LEE HENDRIE ON 8 MARCH, 1998

OPPOSITE PAGE: BATTLING BOLTON'S ALAN THOMPSON ON 12 MAY, 1998

Dion Dublin

COVENTRY CITY

"I'm not a nasty player, but I won't shirk a tackle or a challenge. I just don't go out there intent on smashing people about."

Making your international debut is always special, but to play for your country after having suffered a serious injury earlier in your career makes it doubly so. Little wonder then, that when Dion Dublin – who experienced the agony of a broken leg shortly after joining Manchester United in 1992 – put on an England shirt for the first time last season he was smiling like the cat who has got the cream (plus a very large bowl of Whiskas).

"I was very nervous," said the Coventry forward afterwards, "but it was a nice nervousness because I'd worked hard for it all my career. Just to be in that top and walk out and hear everyone shouting, then sing the national anthem. It was brilliant. I loved every minute of it."

Dublin's debut, against a Salas-inspired Chile, may have ended in defeat but the versatile Sky Blue (he can play with equal aplomb in the heart of defence) received good reviews for his tireless and intelligent performance.

His international call-up was the reward for a season in which Dublin proved himself to be one of the most prolific strikers in the Premiership. Deadly in the air and surprisingly tricky on the floor for a big man, the Marvin Hagler-lookalike's consistent form was a main reason why Coventry fans spent the second part of the season dreaming about a UEFA Cup place – rather than worrying, as they normally do, about relegation.

Despite persistent rumours linking Dublin with bigger and more glamorous clubs, he is adamant that his future still lies at Highfield Road. "The feeling within the club is just brilliant," he says. "I wouldn't want to play anywhere else."

Off the field Dublin relaxes by playing the sax and, last year, demonstrated his musical prowess on Ian Wright's TV show. "It was the most nerve-wracking TV appearance I've ever done," says the budding jazzman. "When I had to do it for real, it took four takes! But it was a great experience for me. I'm still learning, I've only taken it seriously in the last two years." Premiership defenders have been taking Dion Dublin seriously for a lot longer than that.

Age	29
Date of Birth	22.4.69
Birthplace	Leicester
Nickname	Saxo
Position	Striker (and emergency centre-half)

Games & Goals
Cambridge United 156 (52)
Manchester United 12 (2)
Coventry City 135 (58)

Transfers
August 1992 – Cambridge United to Manchester United (£1m)
September 1994 – Manchester United to Coventry City (£2m)

Honours
Division Three Championship 1991

THIS PAGE: VERSATILITY IS DUBLIN'S GREAT FORTE

OPPOSITE PAGE: IN CONTROL AGAINST SHEFFIELD WEDNESDAY, 8 MARCH 1998

Rio Ferdinand

WEST HAM UNITED

"If I could be anybody I'd be rap star Puff Daddy – I love that sort of music."

A few too many bottles of hooch nearly put paid to Rio Ferdinand's England career before it began. Called up for the World Cup qualifier against Moldova last season, the young West Ham defender almost waved goodbye to his international future when he was stopped by police for drink-driving.

Sent home from the squad in disgrace, Ferdinand had time to reflect on the error of his ways. "There won't be any more silly or stupid behaviour from me because I know what's at stake now," he said afterwards. "I'm not going to allow anything to get in the way of being successful."

He was as good as his word. The new-style, squeaky-clean, cola-sipping Ferdy went on to make an international debut against Cameroon which was so polished it could·have been sponsored by Mr Sheen. His composed manner and distribution skills even provoked comparisons with Bobby Moore. "It's great to be compared to Bobby, he is a legend," says the Peckham-born centre-back.

Little wonder, then, that great things are expected of the lad whose potential was so huge Terry Venables had him training with with his Euro 96 squad at the tender age of 17. "He's very special, the best I've seen for a long time," says West Ham youth coach Peter Brabrook. "Better judges than me believe he is a future England captain and who am I to argue with them?"

Certainly, Ferdinand already possesses the typical captain's temperament – steely, focused and positive. "You must have confidence in your own ability and determination," he says, referring to his Jack-like ascent up soccer's beanstalk. "You need to have a strong attitude and commit yourself totally to what you are doing."

This season Ferdinand's commitments will surely include starring roles in England's Euro 2000 qualifying campaign and West Ham's first European adventure since Brooking, Bonds and Co last flashed their passports at Stansted Airport. Looking further ahead, Rio – the cousin of Tottenham's Les – admits that he'd like to test his skills against continental strikers on a more regular basis. "One day I will consider going abroad," he says. "If I was to get the opportunity I would definitely think about it."

Age
19

Date of Birth
7.11.78

Birthplace
Peckham

Nickname
Ferdy

Position
Defender

Games & Goals
West Ham United 51 (2)

Transfers
None

Honours
None

THIS PAGE: HEADING THE BALL FOR WEST HAM ON 24 SEPTEMBER, 1997

OPPOSITE PAGE: CHALLENGED BY BLACKBURN'S GARY FLITCROFT ON 14 FEBRUARY, 1998

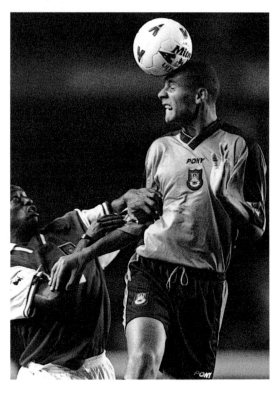

Duncan Ferguson

EVERTON

"I don't think I've cracked it yet. Never say you've done it unless you're one of the top, top players."

Age		
26		
	Date of birth	
	27.12.71	**Birthplace**
		Stirling
Nickname		
Duncan Disorderly		
	Position	
	Striker	
Games & Goals		
Dundee United 77 (27), Rangers 14 (2)		
Everton 103 (34)		
Transfers		
July 1993 –Dundee United to Rangers (£4m)		
October 1994 – Rangers to Everton (£4,4m)		
	Honours	
Scottish League 1994		
Scottish League Cup 1994, FA Cup 1995		

THIS PAGE: AGGRESSIVE INSTINCTS, HEIGHT AND SUBTLE BALL SKILLS MAKE FERGUSON A WINNER

OPPOSITE PAGE: CONFRONTING CHELSEA'S MICHAEL DUBARRY FOR THE BALL, 18 JANUARY, 1998

But for Duncan Ferguson, Everton supporters might have spent much of this year poring over their road maps, working out the best way to get to such football backwaters as Crewe, Bury and Swindon. Thankfully for the blue half of Merseyside, Big Dunc's goals helped Everton avoid the drop last season and allowed their fans to look forward, once again, to Premiership football.

After his starring role in preventing Everton's annual flirtation with relegation from developing into a full-blown affair, Ferguson should have been contemplating a summer in France, playing for Scotland in the World Cup. Instead he was preparing for his wedding in Las Vegas, having announced his "retirement" from international football.

That was just another controversial episode in the career of the player the tabloids call "Duncan Disorderly". In 1995 Ferguson was sent to Barlinnie prison for three months for head-butting Raith Rovers' John McStay. It was not the first time the former Rangers player had been on the wrong side of the law, either – he has three other convictions for assault, one for head-butting a policeman.

On the pitch, though, it is opposition centre-halves who have to contend with the aggressive instincts of the Stirling-born centre-forward. With his height (at 6 ft 4 ins he is one of the tallest players in the Premiership), physical presence and surprisingly subtle ball skills Ferguson is a handful for any defence.

Everton manager Howard Kendall knows how important Ferguson is to his team. On one occasion last season – when Ferguson was out injured – he described his attack as "toothless". With the big Scotsman back in the side, however, The Toffees' frontline looked like it could do battle with a toothy back four consisting of Jaws, Gnasher, Dracula and Ken Dodd.

Commitment, determination, persistence – what you see is what you get with Duncan Ferguson. He even wears his love for Everton on his sleeve – or rather his arm – in the form of a tattoo of a No. 9 above the club's motto (Nil Satis Nisi Optimum). Translated into English that means "nothing but the best", which is what Everton get from Big Dunc every Saturday.

Robbie Fowler

LIVERPOOL

> "If I get two chances, I know I will score one goal."

THIS PAGE: AERIAL DUEL WITH SOUTHAMPTON'S KEN MONKOU, 7 FEBRUARY, 1998

OPPOSITE PAGE: BACK TO FORM THIS COMING SEASON?

To say that last season was a disappointment for Robbie Fowler is a bit like saying Brian Laudrup is not short of a bob or two. Sadly, the Toxteth Terror's campaign was little short of a catastrophe: first, persistent rumours about his private life appeared to affect his normally dead-eyed marksmanship; then, a serious injury in the Merseyside derby ended his hopes of playing in the World Cup; finally, the Liverpool forward had to watch from the sidelines as the precocious Michael Owen replaced him as The Kop's favourite son and grabbed his England squad place.

The first clear signs that all was not well with the "Spice Boy" striker appeared early in the New Year. The goals had dried up and Fowler was reported as having sessions with Eileen Drewery, the faith healer who counselled Glenn Hoddle during his marriage break-up.

It was the first real crisis of Fowler's career. But a quick glance at the record books – he is, after all, the fastest player to 100 goals in Liverpool's history – suggests there is every reason to suppose that the Anfield goal machine will be back to his best net-bulging form this season.

Former Liverpool legend Ian Rush certainly thinks so. "He is already one of the best around but his game is still developing," says Rushie. "We don't know how good Robbie will become."

Far from seeing Michael Owen as a rival to Fowler, Rush thinks the hotshot pair could form one of the game's most prolific double-acts. "The prospect of Robbie and Michael Owen forming Liverpool's strike partnership for the next ten years must make them the envy of every club," says Liverpool's highest-ever scorer. "I can also see them as partners in some future World Cup. Now that is a mouth-watering prospect."

It is also a prospect, no doubt, that appeals to England's youngest player this century. "I would put Robbie up there with someone like Alan Shearer," says Owen. "He's as good a finisher as there is." Nice to know that the new kid on the goalscoring block still has a good word for his mentor.

Paul Gascoigne
MIDDLESBROUGH

> *"I've left clubs before, but I've never been so sad about leaving a club."*
>
> *Gascoigne on leaving Rangers*

Age
31

Date of Birth
27.5.67

Birthplace
Gateshead

Nickname
Gazza

Position
Midfielder

Games & Goals
Newcastle United 92 (21)
Tottenham Hostspur 92 (19), Lazio 41 (6)
Glasgow Rangers 54 (27)
Middlesbrough 7 (0)

Transfers
July 1988 – Newcastle United to
            Tottenham Hotspur (£2m)
May 1992 – Tottenham to Lazio (£5,5m)
June 1995 – Lazio to
            Glasgow Rangers (£4,5m)
March 1998 – Glasgow Rangers to
            Middlesbrough (£3m)

Honours
FA Cup Winner 1991 (Tottenham Hotspur)
Scottish Championship winner 1996, 1997
(Rangers)
Scottish Cup winner 1996 (Rangers)
Scottish League cup winner 1997
(Rangers)

THIS PAGE: OLDER, WISER? GAZZA'S INTO THE SECOND HALF OF HIS CAREER

OPPOSITE PAGE: EVADING A CHALLENGE FROM SHEFFIELD'S BOBBY FORD ON 7 APRIL, 1998

When Paul Gascoigne last played in English football's top flight – for Tottenham, back in 1991 – it was still called Division One, Manchester City were a leading club and there were just as many Martians as Italians in the league (ie none).

In much the same way, the Paul Gascoigne who makes his Premiership debut with Middlesbrough this season will not be the same player as the Gazza of the early 1990s. Then he was a brilliant, madcap, reckless phenomenon; the new-style 31 year-old Gazza, on the other hand, is an altogether steadier individual.

That, at least, is the opinion of Bryan Robson, who paid Rangers £3 million last March to bring the former enfant terrible of English football to the Riverside. "We are getting him at his most mature and his most experienced," says the Boro boss, confidently. "When a player reaches the age of 30 he becomes aware of the fact that he is into the second part of his career and works hard to make sure that he plays for as long as he can."

What, though, about Gazza's reputation for carousing, boozing and causing general mayhem wherever he goes? "I am sure he will give me a little bit of grief from time to time," admits Robson, "but it will be worth it. Paul takes a few pints now and again but he is one of the hardest trainers I have worked with. The other players will see how hard he works."

If he stays injury-free and controls his still-suspect temperament, Gascoigne has the ability to help Middlesbrough finally establish themselves in the Premiership. According to no less an authority than Johan Cruyff, meanwhile, he can also play a key role in England's upcoming European Championship campaign. "Gascoigne is very important to England," says the Dutch legend. "He's like Cantona or Ginola. He doesn't need to play for 90 minutes. He can play half-an-hour here, and 30 minutes there. That's how Glenn Hoddle should use him." Europe beware – after Gazza the superstar, Gazza the clown and Gazza the crock, Gazza the supersub is coming!

Ryan Giggs
MANCHESTER UNITED

"If you nutmeg someone it's humiliating for them so you can guarantee the next time you do it, he's going to kick you."

"Ryan Giggs, Ryan Giggs, flying down the wing!" shout the Manchester United faithful whenever the number 11 does something good, which is rather a lot. The thing is, nowadays Giggs does a good deal more than simply fly down the wing. He has matured into a pretty good imitation of the perfect midfielder, having worked hard on his defensive responsibilities to supplement the main reason he's in the United team – to run the opposition ragged.

Giggs' importance to Manchester United cannot be understated, and it is no coincidence that the Reds' dramatic loss of form (when the club suffered a string of Premiership defeats and were dumped out of the European Cup by Monaco) occurred immediately the Welshman suffered a serious hamstring injury and was forced to sit out two months of the season.

Sometimes it's hard to believe that Giggs is still only 24, he's been around that long. He was blooded by Alex Ferguson as a raw 17-year-old in March 1991, and has been a favourite of the fans since. On his second appearance later that season, he scored the only goal in the Manchester derby and started being compared to the great George Best.

Like Best, Giggs combined glittering feet with dazzling good looks, making both men and (a long string of beautiful) women go weak at the knees. But unlike Best he hasn't let it go to his head. He's let his firmly-on-the-ground-feet do the talking and shied away from publicity as much as you can when you're a young good-looking millionaire. Becoming a father can only make him more settled.

Not that he'll ever get rid of his on-pitch flamboyance, however hard he works at improving his defensive game. "It's chilling the way Ryan seems to float over the surface rather than run like the rest of us," says manager Alex Ferguson. "So light on his feet and blessed with wonderful, wonderful balance."

Former United boss Ron Atkinson is even more fulsome in his praise.

"I would break the bank to buy him," he says. "He makes you believe that there is a football God after all."

Age	
24	
	Date of Birth
	29.11.73
	Birthplace
	Cardiff
Nickname	
Giggsy	
	Position
	Midfielder
Goals & Games	
Manchester United 236 (50)	
Transfers	
None	
	Honours
Premiership 1993, 1994, 1996, 1997	
FA Cup 1994, 1996, League Cup 1992	

THIS PAGE: GIGGSY, THE PERFECT MIDFIELDER

OPPOSITE PAGE: LIGHT ON HIS FEET AGAINST LIVERPOOL ON 6 DECEMBER, 1997

David Ginola

TOTTENHAM HOTSPUR

> "I read Batman and Superman. They are superheroes. But not a footballer, because it is my job. My hero is my boy."

Age
31

Date of birth
25.1.67

Birthplace
Gassin, France

Nickname
El Magnifico

Position
Midfielder/forward

Games & Goals
Toulon 81 (4), Racing Paris 61 (8)
Brest 50 (10), Paris St Germain 125 (34)
Newcastle 58 (6), Tottenham 34 (6)

Transfers
Toulon to Racing Paris
Racing Paris to Brest
Brest to Paris St Germain
Paris St Germain to Newcastle (£2.5m)
Newcastle to Tottenham (£2m)

Honours
French championship 1993/4
(Paris St Germain)
French Cup 1993 and 1995
(Paris St Germain)

THIS PAGE: DAVID GINOLA – RACING TO AVOID RELEGATION

OPPOSITE PAGE: THE SPURS PIN-UP BOY WITH EXTRAVAGANT SKILLS

Last season the form of lanky-haired French flankman David Ginola was just about the only ray of brightness for a miserable Tottenham, and if they're going to avoid another calamitous campaign Christian Gross will be praying he carries on where he left off last May.

There were times in the last season when Ginola appeared to be waging a one-man campaign to save Tottenham from the catastrophe of relegation to Division One. Playing in an injury-ravaged team lacking confidence and discipline, the flamboyant Frenchman still managed to parade the full repertoire of his extravagant skills while at the same time showing a commitment to the club's cause that surprised many of his former critics.

It was all a long way from Ginola's first two years in England, when his sublime wing-play captured the hearts of the Toon faithful as Keegan's Newcastle attempted to wrest the title from Old Trafford in a blaze of attacking football. And while the Spurs of old would have been another natural home for the stylish Ginola, the former French international was joining a crisis-ridden outfit on its way to becoming the laughing stock of London.

"He impressed me tremendously," said former Tottenham legend Dave MacKay after one dazzling Ginola performance. "And not just by doing the things everybody knows he is good at. His all-round game and contribution to the team was excellent."

The Spurs star – who manager Christian Gross tried out in a number of different roles including striker and central midfielder – even won praise from Alan Sugar, despite the Tottenham chairman's well-publicized aversion to "Carlos Kickaball" foreigners. "David is running around, working his heart out and not being supported by colleagues," he pontificated in an address to the Cambridge Union.

Perhaps Ginola's magnificent start to his Spurs career could simply be explained by a desire not to be bored. "I have been relegated once when I was with Racing Paris ten years ago and it's boring," says the pin-up boy of White Hart Lane. His search for thrills even extended to toying with the idea of giving up football and becoming a motor-racing driver, but fortunately for Spurs he decided the excitement of playing football and advertising shampoo was enough.

John Hartson

WEST HAM UNITED

> "I have to give 100 per cent and if that means I've got to kick someone to get the ball, so be it."

Age	23
Date of Birth	5.4.75
Birthplace	Swansea
Nickname	Hart Man
Position	Striker
Games & Goals	Luton 54 (11), Arsenal 53 (14) West Ham 43 (20)
Transfers	January 1995 – Luton to Arsenal (£2,5m) February 1997 – Arsenal to West Ham (£3,2m)
Honours	None

THIS PAGE: WEST HAM'S DANGEROUS CENTRE FORWARD

OPPOSITE PAGE: BEATING BLACKBURN'S DESPERATE COLIN HENDRY TO THE BALL ON 18 APRIL, 1998

It may not be politically correct to say so, but John Hartson is proof positive that redhead equals hothead. Towards the end of last season the irascible ginger nut was publicly labelled "an idiot" by West Ham manager Harry Redknapp, after he threw a punch at Derby's Igor Stimac and was promptly shown the red card.

It was the second time in six games that the carrot-topped centre-forward had first use of the showers (he was also sent off at Bolton for elbowing an opponent). When he managed to stay on the pitch, though, Hartson showed himself to be a danger to any defence, and finished the season as one of the Premiership's leading scorers.

The Welshman is the first to admit that he does not find it easy to keep his cool: "On the pitch I think I've got a bit of a temper which I have to try and control. It's the lads, you see, they get me going in the changing room. They say 'Come on, let them know what you're about', stuff like that. I have to be fired up for a game, or they won't get 100 per cent out of me. But it can take me over the edge."

Despite his suspect temperament – and that very public reprimand – the Swansea-born striker is still a great favourite of Harry Redknapp's. "Hartson is so strong," says the Hammers boss. "He's just frightening. He's an old-fashioned centre forward who goes in where it hurts – sees no fear. When he goes for a cross he doesn't care if he, the ball and his opponent all end up in the back of the net. What a handful for defenders!"

This season it won't only be Premiership defenders who will be battling against the strapping six footer, either. Hartson will be leading West Ham's frontline in their bid for European glory and will be a key weapon in Wales' European championship campaign. Playing for his country means everything to the patriotic Hartson, a fluent Welsh speaker. "The biggest thing I've done up to now in football is to play for Wales," he says.

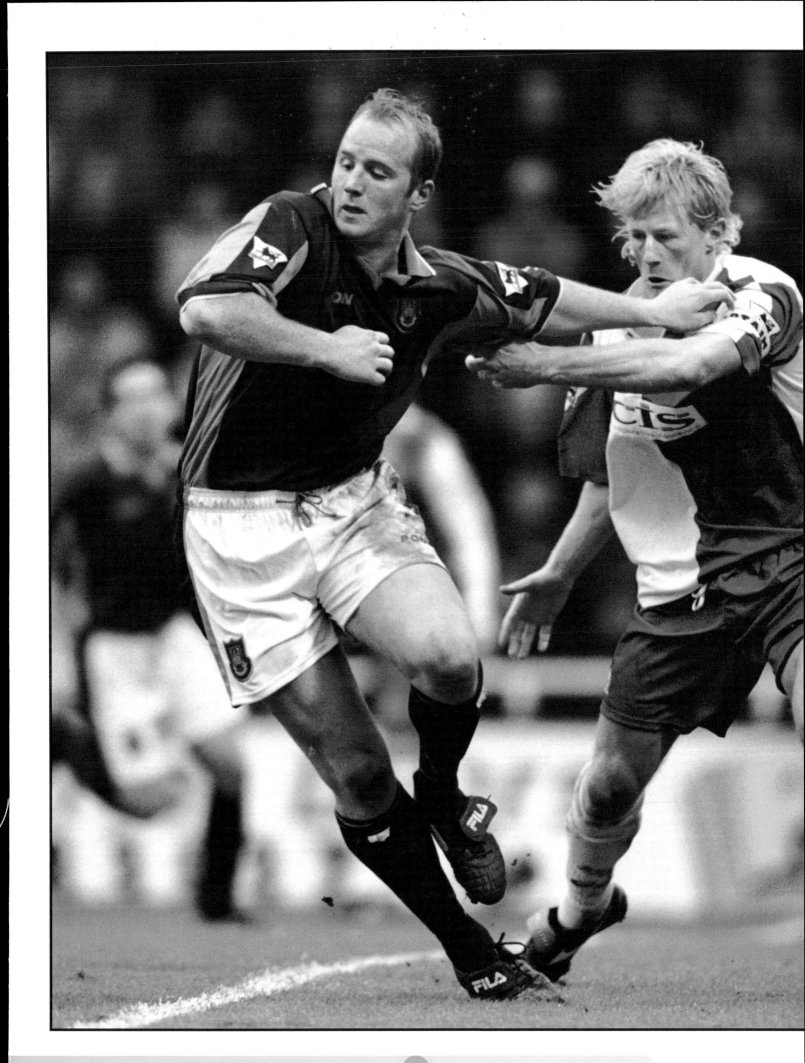

Emile Heskey

LEICESTER CITY

> "I always wanted to be a professional footballer and it never occurred to me that I wouldn't fulfil that ambition."

Age
20

Date of birth
11.1.78

Birthplace
Leicester

Nickname
Bruno

Position
Forward

Games & Goals
Leicester City 101 (27)

Transfers
None. Signed professional forms from trainee in July 1996

Honours
Coca-Cola Cup 1997

THIS PAGE: HESKEY, THE TERROR OF PREMIERSHIP DEFENDERS

OPPOSITE PAGE: PACE, POWER AND COMMITMENT IN MOTION

When Glenn Hoddle called Emile Heskey up for the full England squad last season his father, Tyrone, could be forgiven for feeling a mixture of emotions: pride, at the thought of his son wearing the famous white shirt, but also frustration at having failed some years ago to back his judgement and accept a bookie's odds of 1,000 to 1 against Emile representing England at all levels.

"If only I'd placed that £20 bet I'd have been laughing all the way to the bank," says Heskey senior. "I told his mum when he was 14 he'd be the best in the country and £20,000 is a small price to pay for Emile proving me right." Well, young Heskey may not yet be the nation's top striker but if he can maintain his form and progress of the last three seasons he may yet justify his dad's billing.

Heskey's pace, power, and strength make him one of the most awkward customers for Premiership defenders, and last season he gave more than one centre-half a torrid time. Strangely, however, for a player who possesses all the natural assets a striker could wish for, Heskey joined Leicester as a defender. Youth team coach David Nish soon realized, though, that the youngster's ideal position was up front. And once Heskey had been thrown into first-team action – making his debut against QPR in March 1995 – he rapidly made himself indispensable.

Heskey helped The Foxes win promotion in his first full season and the following year, 1996/97, was even better for the man the Leicester fans call "Bruno" (because he looks a bit like the boxer, but packs a bigger punch), as he rifled in a career-best 12 goals, including the last-ditch Wembley equalizer in the Coca-Cola Cup Final against Middlesbrough. If this season he continues to terrorize Premiership defences with his lethal combination of brute force, searing pace and a deceptively skilfull touch then there's plenty of defenders who'll feel like they'll have gone 12 rounds at 4.45pm on a Saturday afternoon.

Paul Ince

LIVERPOOL

"I wouldn't want to play anywhere just to keep playing. I'd want to go out at the top."

Age	
30	
Date of Birth	
21.11.67	
	Birthplace
	Ilford
Nickname	
The Guv'nor	
	Position
	Midfielder

Games & Goals
West Ham United 72 (6)
Manchester United 206 (24)
Inter Milan 54 (10)
Liverpool 31 (8)

Transfers
September 1989 – West Ham United to Manchester United (£1m)
July 1995 – Manchester United to Inter Milan (£8m)
July 1997 – Inter Milan to Liverpool (£4,2m)

Honours
FA Cup 1990, 1994
European Cup Winners' Cup 1991
League (Rumblelows) Cup 1992
Premiership 1993, 1994

THIS PAGE: TAKING ON NEWCASTLE'S DEFENCE ON 19 JANUARY, 1998

OPPOSITE PAGE: GIVING EVERTON A HARD TIME ON 18 OCTOBER, 1997

Even if he captains a World XI against a team of bug-eyed ball-players from the planet Zog, the image most football fans will forever keep of Paul Ince is from Rome 1997. Fists clenched, blood dripping onto his shirt from a head wound, the snarling, snapping England captain epitomized the determination of Glenn Hoddle's men to take the quickest and most direct route to the World Cup finals.

Ince's gutsy performance that evening elevated him to the position of a national hero. Dubbed "Captain Courage" by the tabloids, the Liverpool midfielder's intelligent, forceful and committed display was probably his best ever in an England shirt.

"Paul Ince was absolutely magnificent," said Glenn Hoddle after the game.

But, then again, he usually is. In a career with West Ham, Manchester United, Inter Milan and now Liverpool Ince has rarely performed below par, and he has a shelf-full of medals for his efforts. By his own high standards, however, last season was a tad disappointing for the player who likes to be called "The Guv'nor". His own form was more up-and-down than normal, contributing to yet another season of under-achievement by The Reds.

All the same, there is no doubt that Ince has the ability to lead Liverpool to greater things this season. "Paul is a top-class player," says Roy Hodgson, Ince's former manager at Inter, "and I am not talking in Premiership terms, I am talking in European terms. He is an excellent player and a good character. You need someone to get a grip on the game, he is capable of doing that. He has honed his attacking skills after two years in the Italian league, and defensively, he is one of the best midfielders in Europe."

One man who won't disagree with that assessment is Don Purkiss, who discovered the young Ince and recommended him to West Ham. "He could play anyway – he was even brilliant in goal," he remembers. "Before too long I told him: 'You'll captain England.'"

Of course, football's answer to Mystic Meg was dead right.

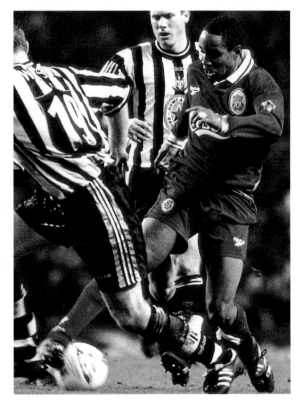

Brian Laudrup

CHELSEA

"Even when I was seven or eight, I couldn't just go out and enjoy my football because everybody was saying, 'There is mini-Laudrup.'"

Age
29

Date of Birth
22.2.69

Birthplace
Vienna, Austria

Nickname
None

Position
Striker

Games & Goals
Brondy 49 (13), Bayer Uerdingen 34 (6)
Bayern Munich 33 (9), Fiorentina 31 (5)
AC Milan (loan), Rangers 116 (33)

Transfers
July 1997 – Rangers to Chelsea (free)

Honours
Danish Championship 1987, 1988
Danish Cup 1989
Scottish Premiership 1995, 1996, 1997
Scottish Cup 1996
Scottish League Cup 1997

THIS PAGE: LAUDRUP AS A CALM RANGER

OPPOSITE PAGE: COMING SOON TO A CHELSEA GAME NEAR YOU

Scottish defenders could have been forgiven for treating themselves to a dram or two of the hard stuff on July 1st, the day Brian Laudrup left Rangers for Chelsea. After four years of being run ragged by the quicksilver Dane they were entitled to a modest celebration.

Before he left Glasgow the joke amongst Rangers fans was that Laudrup had sold so many dummies he was thinking of setting up a branch of Mothercare. Quite simply, the Vienna-born striker had too many tricks for defenders unused to marking a player of genuine world-class standing.

Little wonder, then, that when Laudrup announced the end of his Scottish sojourn the queue of clubs hoping to sign him was longer than the line outside Harrod's at the start of the January sales. Among the top outfits chasing his signature were Paris St Germain and Ajax, the club his older brother, Michael, plays for.

In the end, though, Laudrup plumped for Chelsea. "I want to play in the English Premiership," he says, "and that is what attracted me to Chelsea. They are obviously ambitious but they are also extremely nice people." Nothing to do with the £75,000 a week he'll earn then.

Money aside, however, feeling comfortable with the people around him is extremely important to Laudrup. "I am really happy playing football, going out and performing, giving a lot of joy, hopefully, to the fans... but I can only do that if I'm happy off the pitch," he says.

His relaxed approach to the game, meanwhile, explains why he never appears flustered on the pitch. "I've never seen football as just a job, because it's always been a hobby for me. If there comes a day when I have to get up in the morning and I am only thinking about the money, then I'll pack up."

Laudrup admits he came close to quitting the game during a miserable spell in Italy with Fiorentina and AC Milan. "There was a point when I said, if this is football then it's not the football that I once loved and enjoyed," he recalls. Chelsea fans, no doubt, will be hoping Laudrup enjoys his football at Stamford Bridge.

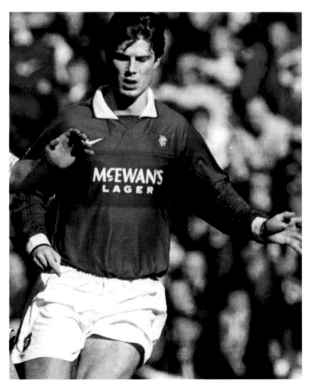

Graeme Le Saux

CHELSEA

> "I am who I am. People tend to forget that my passion as a youngster was to be a footballer and that hasn't changed."

Age
29

Date of Birth
17.10.68

Birthplace
St. Pauls (Jersey)

Nickname
Bergerac, Soxy

Position
Defender/midfielder

Games & Goals
Chelsea 90 (8), Blackburn Rovers 129 (7)
Chelsea 26 (1)

Transfers
Chelsea to Blackburn – player exchange
Blackburn to Chelsea (£5m)

Honours
Premiership 1994/5 (Blackburn Rovers)
Coca Cola Cup 1998 (Chelsea)

THIS PAGE: AT THE PEAK OF HIS CAREER

OPPOSITE PAGE: JUMPING FOR THE BALL AGAINST WIMBLEDON'S NEIL ARDLEY ON 26 DECEMBER, 1997

"Never go back", they say, but Graeme Le Saux ignored that piece of time-honoured advice when he returned to Chelsea at the start of last season four years after leaving Stamford Bridge for Blackburn Rovers.

The exchange deal which took the Jersey-born player to Ewood Park in March 1993 was probably the most lop-sided in English transfer history – Blackburn gained a future England international and a key member of their 1994/95 Premiership-winning squad; Chelsea recruited journeyman striker Steve Livingstone, who made just one substitute appearance for The Blues.

Clearly, the Londoners boobed quite spectacularly. "Selling Le Saux was a mistake which has taken five million pounds to rectify," admits Colin Hutchinson, Chelsea's Managing Director.

Le Saux – known as Bergerac to his teammates because of his Jersey origins – immediately showed himself to be equally at home at left-back or raiding down the left side of midfield in a 4–4–2 formation.

Of course, unlike most of the other players lured to Chelsea as former manager Ruud Gullit trawled the world for talent, Le Saux had the advantage of knowing something about the set-up at Stamford Bridge. "It's reassuringly familiar but refreshingly different," he says. "It's different from the Chelsea that I left because the club have really progressed in the last four years and I've progressed as well."

That personal progression has seen the spikey-haired Le Saux establish himself as a fixture in Glenn Hoddle's England side – this time as an attacking wing-back. A combination of swashbuckling attacking play and never-say-die defending have made him the epitome of the modern-day wide player, the complete article.

Now at the peak of his career, he seems certain to pick up more medals and honours over the next few years. That is as long as he manages to control a quick temper which once saw him smack then Blackburn teammate David Batty in the face during a Champions League match in Moscow and, on another occasion, throw his shirt at former Chelsea manager Ian Porterfield in disgust at being substituted.

Matt Le Tissier

SOUTHAMPTON

"I run out for every match expecting to play well and score a great goal. That confidence has never changed."

L ike Chris Evans, The Spice Girls and The Millennium Dome, Matt Le Tissier divides the nation – for some he's a footballing genius, for others he's a big girl's blouse. Le Tiss, say his critics, is fat, lazy, inconsistent, maddening, arrogant, complacent, unambitious and has very big ears. Strangely, perhaps, his supporters would agree with most of that list, but they'd also add a few words of their own: entertaining, brilliant, imaginative, magical and a scorer of unbelievably exhilarating goals. Oh, and his ears aren't that big either.

Last season was make or break time for the enigmatic Southampton star as he tried to establish himself in Glenn Hoddle's England squad in the run-up to the World Cup. Sadly, injuries and a lapse in form meant that by the time the season finished Le Tissier's chances of making the hop across the Channel were about as high as Bill Clinton keeping his trousers zipped in a Sultan's harem.

The Channel Islander had desperately wanted to play in the World Cup. So much so, in fact, that he arranged a series of meetings with a top sports psychologist in an effort to sort out his mental approach to his game. "I will do everything I can to get back into the England squad", he said at the time. "These days football is not just about playing and fitness, it's just as important to be mentally right and this is certainly helping me."

A self-confessed burger and chocolate addict, Le Tissier also managed to shed half a stone in his bid to appear on the world's largest stage. It was a brave effort but, in truth, it made little difference. A sparkle was lacking in his play and the radar was haywire on those trademark Exocet strikes which used to monopolize "Goal of the Month".

At least Le Tissier's beloved Southampton managed to avoid their customary flirtation with relegation, thanks to some astute signings by rookie manager Dave Jones. Mind you, as far as Saints fans are concerned, Jones could sign Ronaldo, Del Piero or Salas and there would still only be one king of The Dell – Super Matt Le Tiss.

Age
31

Date of Birth
14.10.66

Birthplace
Guernsey

Nickname
God, Le Tiss

Position
Forward

Games & Goals
Southampton 383 (151)

Transfers
None. Signed professional forms from trainee in October 1986

Honours
None

THIS PAGE: LE TISS – KING OF THE DELL

OPPOSITE PAGE: WILL THE NEW SEASON HERALD A RETURN TO TOP FORM?

Steve McManaman

LIVERPOOL

McManaman

"I'm at a place where I've always said I didn't want to leave. I'm thrilled to still be here."

THIS PAGE: SHAGGY – LIVERPOOL'S PRINCIPAL PLAYMAKER

OPPOSITE PAGE: FLYING PAST DERBY TO A 4–0 WIN ON 25 OCTOBER, 1997

Despite struggling to reproduce the form he shows week-in-week out in the red shirt of Liverpool, when he pulls on the white of England, Steve McManaman is still one of the world's most naturally gifted players.

There are few finer sights in football than McManaman picking up the ball on the halfway line, twisting and turning past four or five opponents and firing the ball into the corner of the net. And as Liverpool's key player, it seems that only if he is in this kind of red-hot form this season will the club be good enough to bring the title back to Merseyside after all these years (eight to be exact).

Rejected by a Liverpool boys team, as a youngster Steve McManaman was considered too pasty and lightweight to make it in the beefy world of top-flight football. But while his peers concentrated on their weight training, building themselves up for battle, McManaman stayed outside with the ball at his feet... and developed into one of the most exciting players in the land. But then he's always been different.

It's not just in the way he plays – his spindly body gyrating wildly with the ball seemingly glued to his feet – it's everything about him: his distinctive curly, wavy hair instead of the trademark footballer crop, the baseball cap and old-style football shirt instead of the regulation shell suit, the column in the Times instead of the rant and rave in The People.

McManaman made his debut in a red shirt at the tender age of 18, but it's only over the last couple of seasons that – playing in a free role as Liverpool's principal playmaker – he's really fulfilled his awesome potential and maintained any real consistency, making him an endless source of transfer speculation on the back pages of newspapers in the Barcelona region of Spain.

The one element of his game he knows he could improve on is his goalscoring. Last season he didn't exactly up his rate, but when he did score, boy did he score. His mazy, half-the-length-of-the-pitch runs against Celtic and Aston Villa both ended with the ball in the back of the net where in previous seasons they'd have culminated in a limp shot into the keepers' arms. More of this form would go down well with the fans of both Liverpool and England.

Nigel Martyn

LEEDS UNITED

> "The difference at international level is that you often have less to do, so the saves you do make become more important."

Age
31

Date of birth
11.8.66

Birthplace
St Austell

Nickname
Nige

Position
Goalkeeper

Games & Goals
Bristol Rovers 101, Crystal Palace 272
Leeds United 74 (0)

Transfers
November 1989 – Bristol Rovers to
    Crystal Palace (£1m)
July 1996 – Crystal Palace to
    Leeds United (£2,25m)

Honours
Division Three Championship 1989/90
Zenith Data Systems Cup 1991
Division One Championship 1993/94

THIS PAGE: NIGE – BETTER THAN SEAMAN?

OPPOSITE PAGE: KICKING OFF INTO A
BRIGHT FUTURE

ast season was a strange one for Nigel Martyn. At times he produced some of the best form of his career, helping Leeds press for a place in Europe and earning an international recall in the process.

Commanding, imposing and possessing cat-like agility, the Cornishman appeared the nearest challenger to David Seaman for the England goalie's jersey. Indeed, Martyn's fellow professionals actually rated him higher than the Arsenal keeper, voting him into their PFA Team of the Season.

Unfortunately, there was a flip side. On too many occasions the Leeds keeper committed Grobbelaar-style gaffes more normally associated with Sunday League football than the Premiership. Against Newcastle, for instance, Martyn dived over a 20-yard daisycutter from Ketsbaia to gift the Geordies an equalizer. Worse was to follow at West Ham in March. First, he misjudged a corner, allowing John Hartson an easy tap in at the far post; then a comic misunderstanding with new signing Martin Hiden on the edge of the area let in Samassi Abou for a second soft goal.

Martyn's eccentric performance that evening at Upton Park was worthy of a starring slot on "Beadle's About". Not that Leeds manager George Graham was amused – he publicly blamed his keeper for the defeat. But if Martyn was disappointed with his display, he was very soon able to put it in perspective. Taking off from Stansted airport after the game the Leeds plane crash landed, and the team had to make a dash for the emergency exits. Once they had recovered from their ordeal the joke amongst the Leeds players was that it was the fastest they had seen Martyn move all evening.

Despite his occasional lapses, Martyn is one of the finest goalkeepers in the country. The future looks bright for him, too.

At club level he can look forward to playing in a Leeds side gradually emerging, once again, as genuine title contenders. The dearth of English goalkeepers in the Premiership, meanwhile, means he is likely to figure on the international scene for many seasons yet. The next few years will tell whether he's remembered for his blunders or his blinders.

Paul Merson

MIDDLESBROUGH

> "I am certainly not the kind of guy to run away from a challenge."

THIS PAGE: THE MAGIC MAN – ADDICTED TO SUCCESS

OPPOSITE PAGE: TUSSLING WITH CHELSEA'S GRAEME LE SAUX ON 29 MARCH, 1998

Fabrizio Ravanelli was never the most popular player among his Middlesbrough teammates but Paul Merson, in particular, had special reason to cheer the departure of the White Feather from Teeside. Why?

Well, simply because Ravanelli's move to Marseille last August gave Merson the chance to move into the Italian's old house, and so put an end to his early season commuting nightmare.

"About three weeks after coming here, I didn't like it at all," recalls Merson. "I was depressed with the daily commuting from London and was close to packing the game in altogether." The Magic Man soon perked up once he settled into Rava's gaff, though, and started doing what he does best – terrorising defences with a combination of mazy dribbling, powerful shooting and astute passing.

Merson's form during Middlesbrough's promotion campaign was so hot he won a recall to the England team, starting his first international for four years against Switzerland. He scored England's equalizer, too.

That goal seemed to mark the final stage in Merson's rehabilitation, after his well-publicized battles with alcohol, cocaine and gambling. But it's been a long road to recovery for the player with the foppish Hugh Grant haircut. "You need people all the time to help you through," he says. "I know I couldn't have done it without the support I have received in the recovery rooms. It is a lonely journey to make on your own. I wish I'd found those meetings earlier. I think I could have played 50 times for England. People might think that's big-headed, but it's honest."

Having sorted out his off-field life, the only thing The Merse is addicted to is success with Middlesbrough. "Everyone is rooting for the chance to be back among the big boys," he says. "I didn't come here to sit in the First Division for five years."

Merson's former Arsenal clubmate Niall Quinn, now at Sunderland, is sure he will be a force in the Premiership this season. "He was the outstanding player in the First Division last season," he says. "I don't think he has had a bad game for Boro. He's a credit to football."

Marc Overmars

ARSENAL

> "I am a positive man, I don't let anything phase me. I try to enjoy my football, it is very important."

Marc Overmars, of course, is the first man to get to Nicolas Anelka's back-header. There aren't many who beat him for pace. But the ball's at an awkward height as it bounces towards the penalty box, and there's still Schmeichel to beat. No problem for Overmars whose first touch is to head the ball down into his path, giving him more time and space, and allowing him to shoot. Schmeichel spreads himself, of course, but Overmars has been waiting for this and the second touch slots it through the Danish international's legs and into the Old Trafford net. 1–0. Suddenly, remarkably, Arsenal are back in the title hunt.

Much of Arsenal's late winter form that led to their Championship revival was down to a canny move by Gunners manager Arsene Wenger, who allowed the Dutch international access into the channel between the full back and central defence, rather than confining his harelike runs just to the left wing. Overmars started scoring, and Arsenal started winning (usually 1–0) and you know the rest. "I brought Marc to the club to bring us some extra pace and attacking options, and he has certainly done that," says Wenger of his man. He certainly has.

Overmars took a while to settle into English football after his £5 million signing from Ajax, even longer than his international teammate Dennis Bergkamp, who was branded a flop when he first started playing for Arsenal. "It does take time for the foreign players coming to England to adapt to the different style of play and pace of the game," says the Arsenal number 10 of his attacking partner.

Arsenal fans are delighted to see the return to form of the winger who looked so good for Holland against England in 1993 (remember that penalty he won at Wembley in the World Cup qualifier?) and for Ajax, with whom he won the European Cup against Milan in 1995. For a while they were wondering if it was the same man, and now they're sure. He's Overmars, he's over here, and the Gunners are over the moon about it.

Age
24

Date of Birth
14.6.74

Birthplace
Emst, Holland

Nickname
Roadrunner

Position
Midfielder

Games & Goals
Ajax 178 (36), Arsenal 32 (12)

Transfers
July 1997 – Ajax to Arsenal (£7m)

Honours
Dutch championship 1994, 1995, 1996
European Cup 1995
Premier League, FA Cup 1998

THIS PAGE: ROADRUNNER AT FULL PELT

OPPOSITE PAGE: CHALLENGING BLACKBURN GOALKEEPER ALAN FETTIS-BLACK IN A 50/50 BALL ON A SNOWY 13 APRIL, 1998

Michael Owen

LIVERPOOL

Age		
18		
	Date of Birth	
	14.12.79	
	Birthplace	
	Chester	
Nickname		
None		
	Position	
	Striker	
Games & Goals		
Liverpool 38 (19)		
Transfers		
None		
	Honours	
None		

THIS PAGE: A FAST AND FURIOUS YOUNG PRODIGY

OPPOSITE PAGE: SAILING PAST WIMBLEDON GOALKEEPER NEIL SULLIVAN ON 10 JANUARY, 1998

By any normal reckoning, Michael Owen should be going around with his Premiership L-plates on: making the occasional first-team appearance but otherwise learning his trade in Liverpool's reserve and youth sides. As for playing for England – well, that should merely be the stuff of daydreams while he cleans his boots.

Except Owen is not normal, he is a phenomenon. From the day he made his Liverpool debut – scoring against Wimbledon in May 1997 – the young striker has shown himself to be an extraordinary prospect. Last season the Everton-supporting Owen added achievement to promise, establishing himself in the The Reds' first eleven and going on to win the PFA's Young Footballer of the Year award.

But that was not all. On February 11th, 1998 Owen became the youngest England international this century when he made his debut against Chile, aged 18 years and 59 days. He didn't score, but afterwards expressed satisfaction with his performance: "I thought I did alright on my debut. It was natural that I suffered from a little bit of nerves. But I wasn't overawed at all."

The nerveless Owen immediately won a ringing endorsement from Glenn Hoddle. "He seems to have exactly the right temperament," said the England boss. Other respected figures in the game, meanwhile, have been queuing up to praise the Chester-born prodigy. "He may not be very big but he has proved he can handle the physical side of the game," says Liverpool manager Roy Evans. "He is nobody's kicking boy."

"Michael is sensational," adds former Kop hero John Barnes, "and not just because of his pace. His workrate has always been good but now he holds up the ball better and brings other people into the game."

Despite his undoubted talent, this season could be a difficult one for Owen. Premiership defences will be making special plans for him and expectations – from fans, teammates and the media – will be higher. Typically, though, the young speedster remains unfazed. "At this stage of my career it is vital for me to stay fit, keep learning and keep my feet on the floor," he says.

Emmanuel Petit

ARSENAL

> "I think my brother's death was like a ritual sacrifice for me to be a professional player."

Age
27

Date of Birth
22.9.70

Birthplace
Dieppe, France

Nickname
Manu

Position
Midfielder

Games & Goals
Monaco 222 (4), Arsenal 32 (3)

Transfers
June 1997 – Monaco to Arsenal (£3,5m)

Honours
French Young Player of the Year 1990
French Cup 1991
French championship 1997
Premier League, FA Cup 1998

THIS PAGE: BATTLING BARNSLEY'S NEIL RADFEARN ON 25 APRIL, 1998

OPPOSITE PAGE: ESCAPING CHELSEA'S MARK HUGHES DURING THE COCA COLA SEMI FINAL, 18 FEBRUARY, 1998

His name may translate as "little", but there was nothing undersized about Emmanuel Petit's contribution to Arsenal's Double-chasing season last term. With his French compatriot, the rubber-legged Patrick Vieira, Petit formed a midfield partnership as powerful as any in the Premiership.

Strong in the tackle, determined and competitive, Petit played an instrumental role in The Gunners' storming post-Christmas run which saw them sprint past ailing leaders Manchester United in the league and reach the FA Cup Final. Petit also impressed with his range of passing and – in the last weeks of the season, at least – his eye for goal. Yet the pony-tailed Frenchman admits he struggled at first to get to grips with Premiership football. "When I first joined Arsenal it was very difficult for me to adapt to the English game," recalls Petit. "It is so much more physical and quick than in France."

However, Arsenal boss Arsene Wenger – who used to manage Petit at Monaco – was in no doubt that the midfielder could succeed at Highbury. "I bought Petit for his character and determination, as well as his ability," he says. "You cannot bring a player to Arsenal in midfield if he doesn't have that."

However, at some points last season the man nicknamed Manu lived up to his other moniker – Petit petulant. In particular, his sending off against Aston Villa for pushing referee Paul Durkin raised doubts about his temperament. However, while admitting he was rebellious as a youth (the result, he says, of his brother's tragic death while playing amateur football), Petit now claims he is a lot calmer – thanks to a newly-acquired interest in Buddhism. "I was angry and too often ill at ease with myself and I almost gave up playing," he says. "But I have read a number of books on Oriental philosophy in the hope of achieving inner peace. They have helped me succeed."

This season, as Arsenal's Champions' League campaign takes them to some of Europe's most intimidating venues, Petit will need all the serenity he can muster. Good news, indeed, for the manager of his local Zen Buddhist bookshop.

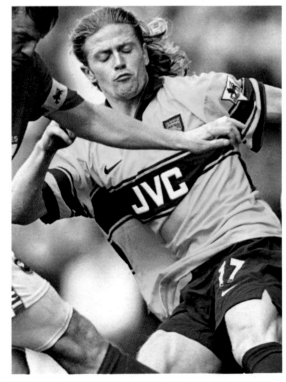

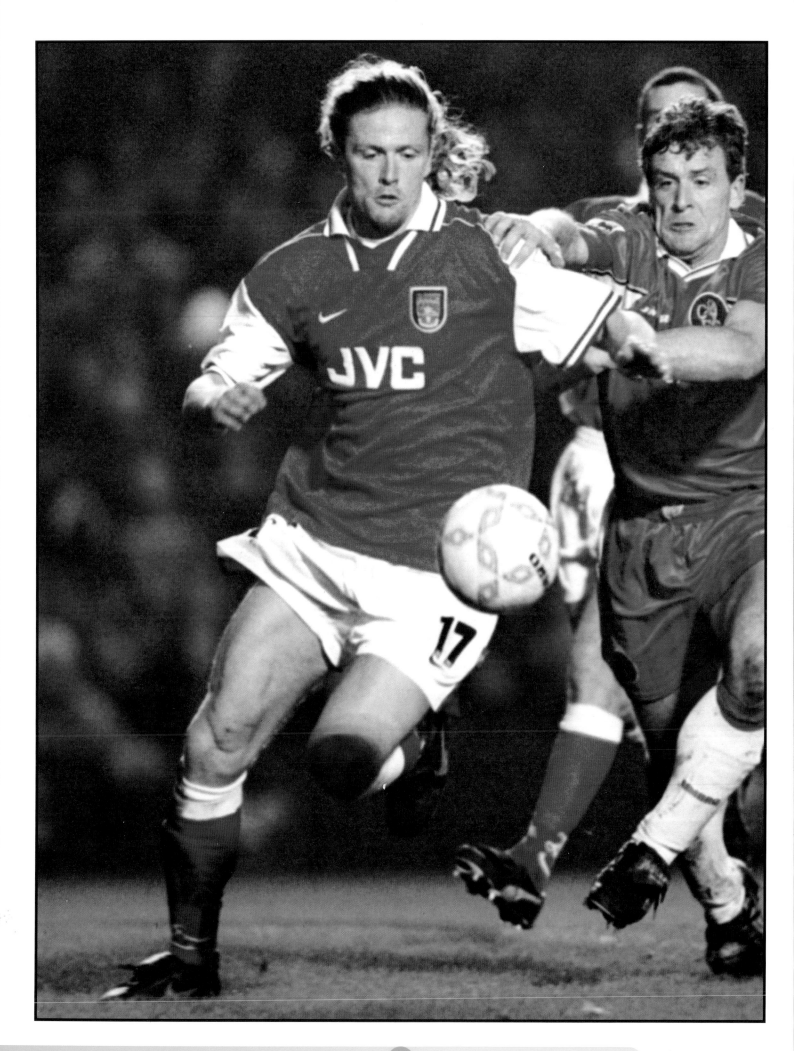

Peter Schmeichel

MANCHESTER UNITED

> "As an older player I'm very happy with the younger players taking all the attention. I've got nothing interesting in life to attract that attention."

Age	34
Date of Birth	18.11.63
Birthplace	Gladsaxe, Denmark
Nickname	The Great Dane
Position	Goalkeeper

Games & Goals
Hvidovre 88 (6), Brondby 119 (2)
Manchester United 258 (0)

Transfers
August 1991 – Brondby to
Manchester United (£550,000)

Honours
Danish Cup 1989
Danish Division One title 1987, 1988, 1989
European Championship 1992
Premiership 1993, 1994, 1996, 1997
FA Cup 1994, 1996
League Cup 1992

THIS PAGE: VOCIFEROUS AND GREAT

OPPOSITE PAGE: THE GREAT DANE
IN ACTION

here are Danes and then there are Great Danes. Then there's Peter Schmeichel. It is very difficult to imagine a better goalkeeper, unless you imagine Schmeichel in a couple of years time – for Manchester United's number one seems to get better and better with age.

After yet another season when the Denmark number one's astonishing ability to keep the ball out of the United goal – defying the laws of velocity, gravity and fairness all in one go – have played a huge part in a United title win, Schmeichel is still the Premiership's, and probably the world's, best.

Schmeichel is a master at spreading his body to thwart an advancing attacker, a trick he learnt being a goalkeeper in a different sport. "I used to be a goalkeeper at handball," he explains. "I've used the star-jump in football all my life. You cover a great deal of the goal but at the same time you can actually watch what is going on. If you were diving and the attackers change to something else, you haven't got a chance to come back."

He is also an expert at stopping shots, agile in the dive and has hand-eye coordination that could have made him a tennis player. Add to all that a masterful technique at cross taking, the ability to score last minute goals in desperate situations (well, he did it once, against Rotor Volgograd in the UEFA Cup in 1995), a sergeant-major-like authority over his defence and you've got one hell of a keeper – arguably the best in the world, undoubtedly (at £550,000 from Brondby in 1991) the best value signing Alex Ferguson has ever made.

Every goalkeeper makes mistakes but Schmeichel makes so few that you can recall just about every one. The biggest blunder of his career came at Old Trafford in the FA Cup in 1998. Trying to boot away a back pass he savagely sliced the ball across his goal, presenting John Hendrie with the sort of chance a six-year-old would have put in. He scored. It was the first goal Manchester United had conceded all season that wasn't followed by a barrage of angry shouting at the defence from the most vocal player in the Premiership.

Paul Scholes

MANCHESTER UNITED

Scholes

> "I don't want to be like any other player. I just want to be myself, not the new Kenny Dalglish."

He's an England international who has been likened to Denis Law, Kenny Dalglish and Eric Cantona, yet Paul Scholes is still not sure of a place in the Manchester United starting eleven. Last season, though, was the most satisfying one yet for the carrot-topped midfielder-cum-striker as he featured in around 75% of The Reds' matches.

After a number of years during which Alex Ferguson seemed reluctant to give the versatile youngster an extended run in the side, the United boss finally gave Scholes the opportunity to parade his skills on a regular basis. Mind you, his claims for a first-team berth were difficult to ignore after Scholes hit the headlines in the summer with a stunning goal against Italy on his full England debut.

Scholes was a surprise package that night – so much so, in fact, that the Italian manager Cesare Maldini wrote up the name "Sholes" on his tactics board (perhaps he'd been listening to soccer commentator Brian Moore, who invariably mispronounces the United star's name).

Back at Old Trafford, nobody worries about how to pronounce Scholes' name – they just call him Archie. Since joining United as a YTS apprentice the jack-in-the-box goal poacher has made an effortless progression through the ranks, earning rave reviews from all the coaches he played under.

"He also has this wonderful passing ability and knack of scoring goals," says Phil Neville, who alongside his brother Gary and Nicky Butt played in the same Sunday side as the young Scholes. "I can honestly say I have never seen Paul have a bad game."

As any Premiership defender could tell you he's no soft touch, either. "Like all great players, Paul has a bit of a nasty streak," says Neville. "Eric Cantona had it. So has Paul. They do not go around kicking people, but they mean it when they play. I can remember when I first came across Paul. We all thought that we could rough up the little kid. Wrong, he always gets you." In short, he's a winner and just the sort of player Glenn Hoddle will need for England's tricky-looking European Championship campaign.

Age
23

Date of Birth
16.11.74

Birthplace
Salford

Nickname
Archie

Position
Midfielder/Striker

Games & Goals
Manchester United 98 (26)

Transfers
None

Honours
Premiership 1996, 1997
FA Cup 1996

THIS PAGE: BEING A SILLY ARCHIE

OPPOSITE PAGE: PRESSING A STRICKEN PAUL INCE OF LIVERPOOL FOR THE BALL, 12 APRIL, 1998

David Seaman

ARSENAL

"I've had my moustache since I was 17 and I'm telling you there's absolutely no chance of me shaving it off!"

Age
34

Date of Birth
19.9.63

Birthplace
Rotherham

Nickname
England's No 1

Position
Goalkeeper

Games & Goals
Leeds 0, Peterborough 91
Birmingham City 75
Queens Park Rangers 141, Arsenal 280 (0)

Transfers
August 1982 – Leeds to Peterborough (£4,000)
October 1984 – Peterborough to Birmingham (£100,000)
August 1986 – Birmingham to QPR (£225,000)
May 1990 – QPR to Arsenal (£1,3m)

Honours
Division One championship 1991
FA Cup 1993, Coca-Cola Cup 1993
European Cup Winners' Cup 1994
Premier League, FA Cup 1998

THIS PAGE: DEFINITELY ENGLAND'S NO 1

OPPOSITE PAGE: POETRY IN MOTION – CLASHING WITH DERBY'S PAOLO WANCHOPE, 29 APRIL, 1998

ast season Arsene Wenger had a problem other managers would sell their grandmothers to have. Alex Manninger, his young Austrian goalkeeper had come into the side when David Seaman was injured, and had not only kept a string of clean sheets but had also picked up the Carling Player of the Month award for March. Seaman, though, was now fit and itching to get back into the Double-chasing Gunners side.

So what did Wenger do? Did he decide it would be foolhardy to change a winning side? Did he, like Gianluca Vialli, opt to play one keeper in the league and another in the cup? Did he hell! Instead, in a display of ruthlessness not seen since Stalin had an ice-pick planted in Trotsky's head, Wenger dropped the brilliant Manninger and put Seaman straight back into the line-up.

Seaman, of course, was as immaculate as ever and immediately helped Arsenal into the FA Cup Final with a string of fine saves against Wolves in the semi. It was just the sort of performance he has been producing season in, season out since he arrived at Highbury from QPR in 1990.

"Seaman is the ultimate student of the game," says Arsenal goalkeeping coach Bob Wilson, "and he never ceases to amaze me in training. Ultimately, you cannot be a goalkeeper without looking as if you belong. David Seaman doesn't always get the praise he deserves because he makes things look so easy. He just belongs."

Seaman's greatest asset, says Wilson, is his upper body strength. "It's the kind of strength that makes the difference between parrying a shot so it hits the post and goes in, and parrying it so that it hits the post and goes to safety. It's that very strength that makes him such a formidable penalty-saver."

Unfortunately, when the whole of the country was willing him to save a spot-kick – against Germany at Euro 96 – Seaman was not so "able". But with Euro 2000 looming and the prospect of more sudden death (or glory) deciders, he may yet have an opportunity to settle an old score.

Alan Shearer

NEWCASTLE UNITED

There was one moment in the rather dull Liverpool v Newcastle match in January 1998 that sticks in the memory. Alan Shearer, just on the pitch off the bench for his second cameo appearance after his injury lay-off, turned on a loose ball only to see Paul Ince bearing down on him – 50-50 ball time, and at some speed. Ince crunched in as only Ince does; Shearer stuck his foot against the ball which span off, lucky not to burst, into touch. The Newcastle forward went flying into the air, and landed. The nation held its breath. Shearer stood up, none the worse for wear, shared a joke with his England team-mate and got on with the game. "Shearer is back!" chanted the Newcastle fans.

They had a right to be happy. Just look what happened to Kenny Dalglish's team in the striker's absence. From title aspirants to relegation-haunted has-beens Newcastle simply couldn't score goals without the England international number nine leading the line. That was one costly ankle injury down Gallowgate way.

Typically, the local lad came good as soon as he had recovered from his pre-season mishap, ahead of schedule, of course. In his first game back he set up that last minute goal against Bolton which led Temur Ketsbaia to go rather overboard with his celebrations. After the Liverpool match he disposed of Stevenage with three goals in the bad-tempered brace of matches between the two clubs. A swashbuckling one yard thumper against Sheffield United was enough to get United into the final of the FA Cup and at least give some positivity to the season from hell.

Shearer's strength is his strength. In an era when football and footballers are changing shape the sheet-metal worker's son is about as close as you can get to the traditional English centre forward: no great dribbler of the ball but a beast with a great header and a thumping shot on him that you wouldn't want to get in the way of even if if you had time to. The only similarity he shares with Mary Poppins (who shamed Toon directors Freddie Sheperd and Douglas Hall allegedly compared him to) is that he's good in the air. And, finally, he's the way England and Newcastle fans want him to be: fighting fit again.

Age	28
Date of Birth	13.8.70
Birthplace	Newcastle
Nickname	Smokey
Position	Striker

Games & Goals
Southampton 118 (23)
Blackburn Rovers 138 (112)
Newcastle United 48 (27)

Transfers
July 1992 – Southampton to Blackburn Rovers (£3,6m)
August 1996 – Blackburn Rovers to Newcastle United (£15m)

Honours
Premiership 1995

THIS PAGE: HUGGED BY STEVENAGE'S MARK SMITH DURING THE MEMORABLE 1–1 DRAW MATCH ON 25 JANUARY, 1998

OPPOSITE PAGE: THE BIG MAN COLLIDES WITH LIVERPOOL'S PHIL BABB ON 19 JANUARY, 1998

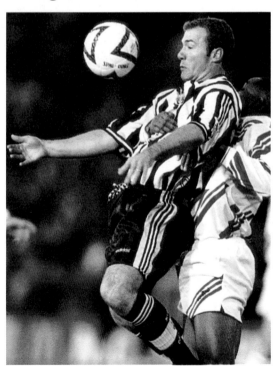

Teddy Sheringham
MANCHESTER UNITED

> "I moved to United in the belief that I could help them win things and suddenly the success dried up."

Age
32

Date of Birth
2.4.66

Birthplace
Highams Park

Nickname
None

Position
Striker

Games & Goals
Millwall 220 (93), Aldershot (loan) 5 (0)
Nottingham Forest 42 (14)
Tottenham Hotspur 166 (76)
Manchester United 31 (9)

Transfers
July 1991 – Millwall to
         Nottingham Forest (£2m)
August 1992 – Nottingham Forest to
         Tottenham Hotspur (£2,1m)
July 1997 – Tottenham Hotspur to
         Manchester United (£3,5m)

Honours
Division Two title 1988

THIS PAGE: A NEW HERO AT UNITED?

OPPOSITE PAGE: EYING THE BALL AT THE CHAMPION'S LEAGUE GAME IN ROTTERDAM ON 5 NOVEMBER, 1997

At the end of the 1996/97 season Manchester United had a big problem. Eric Cantona, darling of the fans and the art director of most of the team's moves, retired. Who, we wondered, could possibly replace the Frenchman? Ronaldo? Del Piero? Laudrup? Er, no, Sheringham actually.

When Alex Ferguson signed Teddy Sheringham to do the job there was more than a little sniggering from the anti-United brigade. Sure Sheringham was an England international and sure he wasn't a bad player. But another Eric Cantona? Paf. The much predicted end of an era, however, never came. Sheringham might not have the effortless style of the Frenchman, but he took to the "in the hole" role like a mallard off the top board.

"Teddy fitted in easily, though he had a spell early on when he didn't quite realize or grasp the intensity of United's games," says his manager of the London-born striker. "Now he has proved himself a terrific replacement for Eric. He is not a twin of Cantona in that they are identical football players. But there are similarities. With both we were and are able to use their outstanding positional play to exploit the talent in the rest of the team."

Going to United was an excellent career move for the England international who, at the age of 31, had never won any major honours in his life. He's not as fast as he was, and he never was very fast, but playing between the midfield and attack requires positional acumen more than speed and Sheringham knows his way round that area of the football pitch like a black cab driver knows his own manor.

So the mourning suits at United have been put back in mothballs and a new hero has emerged. He might not be as exotic as Cantona, but he's just as effective. And he's not likely to give up the game to take up acting, either.

Ole Gunnar Solskjaer

MANCHESTER UNITED

"When I was very young Liverpool used to be my favourite team, but as soon as I joined United I decided never to play for them."

t's amazing that a player can make the sort of impact Ole Gunnar Solskjaer has without people in the game managing to pronounce his name right. His teammates call him Ollie, the usually well-informed Barry Davies calls him Solshire: remarkably the commentator who makes the best crack at it is Brian Moore. Let's once and for all get it straight. The man is called Ool-ah Gunnah Sol-shah. Repeat ten times.

Opposing defenders, of course, have found it equally difficult to fathom out the way the 24-year-old Norwegian ghosts into the box and cracks the ball past their goalkeepers. Such an innocent looking face. Such a slight frame. Such a deadly assassin.

Solskjaer is a master at scoring goals at vital moments in vital matches. Chelsea were minutes away from their second consecutive 2–1 win at Old Trafford last season when Ferguson brought the Norwegian on from the bench he has grown used to warming. He might not be such a secret any more, but he's some weapon to have in reserve. The ball came in from the right, skimmed off Lebouef's shiny pate and fell to United's number 20. With his first touch the striker controlled the ball, with his second he curled it into the top corner. A point saved, a point made. He may be a victim of Ferguson's squad rotation but he'll never be out of the first-team frame.

The goal against Chelsea epitomized the style of the Norwegian international, who, remarkably, was playing Third Division football in his country just four years ago. He is an instinctive goal-scorer whose first instinct is to control the ball (with whatever part of the body comes to hand), and whose second is to smack it past the goalkeeper. He is deadly accurate with his shooting, renowned as being the best player on the training pitch for United.

Solskjaer senior, Ole's dad, was the Norwegian national champion wrestler for many years, and Ole Gunnar – who is actually allergic to grass – could well have followed him into the ring. Opposing defenders wish he had; leaving Manchester United and Norway fans singing Ole-luia because he didn't.

Age		
25	**Date of Birth**	
	26.2.73	**Birthplace**
		Kristiansund, Norway

Nickname
The Baby-faced Assassin

Position
Striker

Games & Goals
Molde 42 (31)
Manchester United 55 (23)

Transfers
July 1996 – Molde to
       Manchester United (£1,5m)

Honours
Premiership 1997

THIS PAGE: CELEBRATION TIME FOR THE BABY-FACED ASSASSIN FROM NORWAY

OPPOSITE PAGE: THE INSTINCTIVE GOAL-SCORER IN CONTROL

Gareth Southgate

ASTON VILLA

> "I've got the rest of my career to do something people will remember me for, rather than forever being the guy who missed a penalty."

Age
27

Date of birth
3.9.70

Birthplace
Watford

Nickname
None

Position
Defender

Games & Goals
Crystal Palace 152 (15)
Aston Villa 91 (2)

Transfers
Crystal Palace to Aston Villa (£2,5m)

Honours
Coca-Cola Cup 1996

Last season Aston Villa captain Gareth Southgate developed a habit which was once associated with the late, great Bobby Moore: turning below-average form at club level around with brilliant performances for his country.

Southgate was outstanding in Rome as England clung on for the draw which secured qualification for the World Cup in France. The much-vaunted Italian strike trio of Zola, Vieri and Inzaghi barely had a shot between them thanks to the stout defending of their English markers, of whom Southgate was probably the pick of the bunch. Before that match, though, the super-cool defender had been struggling to recapture the form which first catapulted him into the national squad in 1996 under Terry Venables.

It didn't help that Aston Villa got off to their worst start in living memory, losing their first four league matches. Nor that Southgate then had a public disagreement with then boss Brian Little about the state of the club and its ambitions for the future. Nevertheless, Southgate still managed to star in Villa's exciting UEFA Cup run, showing once again that he tends to perform best on the biggest of stages.

Southgate is an intelligent, resourceful player who can play either in a back four or as one of three centre-backs, as favoured by England boss Glenn Hoddle. His preference, though, is for the latter. "I'm very comfortable with it," he says. "I enjoy being able to create from defence. It's certainly the way forward and most of our Premiership teams are doing it now."

It's a sad fact that whatever Southgate achieves in the game with club or country, he is still likely to be remembered as the player who missed the vital sudden-death penalty against Germany at Euro 96. Typically, though, the Villa man drew strength from that low moment. "A setback in life can spur you on," he says. "You can shrivel up and sit in a corner and mope about it or you can push ahead and try to do something about the future."

Aston Villa fans will be hoping that means playing just as well for club as for country this season.

THIS PAGE: THE VILLA CAPTAIN IN ACTION

OPPOSITE PAGE: SUPER-COOL DEFENDER

Chris Sutton

BLACKBURN ROVERS

"I've always been a country person. When I retire, I'll live in the country and not see anybody!"

Age
25

Date of Birth
10..3.73

Birthplace
Nottingham

Nickname
The Bostick Twin (with Ruel Fox, while at Norwich)

Position
Striker

Games & Goals
Norwich City 102 (35)
Blackburn Rovers 113 (44)

Transfers
July 1994 –Norwich City to
          Blackburn Rovers (£5m)

Honours
Premiership 1995

t's unusual for a striker to score an own goal, but Chris Sutton managed a spectacular one last season. By refusing to play for England's B team against Chile in February the Blackburn striker effectively ruled himself out of contention for a World Cup place.

Sutton snubbed Hoddle because he felt he deserved a place in the A squad, having just made his England debut as a substitute against Cameroon. Despite blowing his chances of a trip to France – he might just as well have torn up his passport after his bust-up with the England boss – Sutton remains unrepentant.

"It was my decision and I stand by it," he says. "I was not trying to be arrogant. No one would like to play for England more than me. If Glenn Hoddle does not rate me, that's fine. It is his prerogative. But I have played in B games before and I would be on a hiding to nothing."

As for Hoddle, well, it seems unlikely that he'll be storing Sutton's telephone number in his own phone's memory bank. "In the end it's his decision," says the England supremo. "If someone doesn't want to play for their country I won't force them."

Sutton probably has more chance of winning the lottery than he does of figuring in England's European Championship campaign. Nevertheless, he can at least look forward to some overseas adventures with Blackburn in the UEFA Cup.

So what can continental defenders expect when they get to tangle with the Rovers striker? "He is physical, he works hard and he has an eye for goal," says Leicester's Spencer Prior, a former teammate of Sutton's at Norwich. "He is also versatile and can play in several positions. But he has always been his own player and he will play the way he wants. If he is allowed a free role he will express himself. He is very skillful, too, for a big man."

Many of the qualities, in fact, you'd look for in an international player. Unfortunately, Sutton's bold (but surely misconceived) decision to cock a snook at Hoddle means he is likely to remain a long-term outcast from the England camp.

THIS PAGE: STRIKER WITH ATTITUDE

OPPOSITE PAGE: JUMPING ABOVE TOTTENHAM'S SOL CAMPBELL

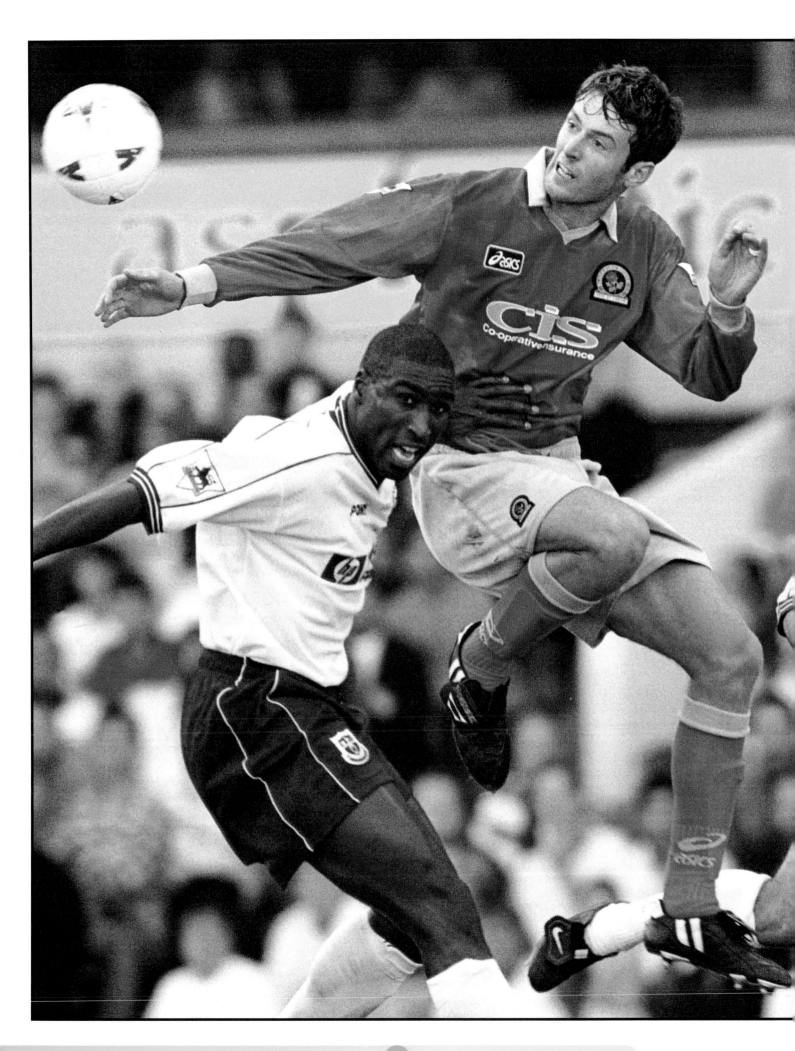

Pierre van Hooijdonk

NOTTINGHAM FOREST

> "People can call me all the names they want, but no-one can say that I am not a good professional and that I don't do my job properly."

Age
28

Date of Birth
29.11.69

Birthplace
Steenbergen, Holland

Nickname
None

Position
Striker

Games & Goals
RBC 69 (33), NAC Breda 99 (71)
Celtic 66 (46), Nottingham Forest 50 (30)

Transfers
January 1995 – NAC Breda to Celtic (£1,2m)
March 1997 – Celtic to
Nottingham Forest (£4,5m)

Honours
Division One Champions 1998

THIS PAGE: LOOKING FOR THE BALL WITH BIRMINGHAM'S MICHAEL JOHNSON, 21 MARCH, 1998

OPPOSITE PAGE: HELD BY BIRMINGHAM'S CHRIS MARSDEN DURING THE SAME MATCH AT ST ANDREW'S

f Pierre van Hooijdonk scores as many goals this season as he did last time round, not only will Forest survive in the Premiership, they will probably be pushing for a UEFA Cup place or maybe, even, challenging for the title.

Without van Hooijdonk it's doubtful that Forest would now be in the top flight. His 30 goals in The Reds' promotion campaign were the main reason why the East Midlanders returned to the Premiership at the first time of asking. Now Forest will be hoping that the deadly Dutchman can be just as prolific against the country's top defences.

Van Hooijdonk, though, is eager to point out that there's a lot more to his game than simply plonking the ball into the net. "I would hate people to judge me just on my scoring record," he says. "I might have the job of striker, but mentally I am an attacking midfield player. If I drop deep, and the defender comes with me, Kevin Campbell can be in a one-against-one situation. You know, I like setting people up, but, really, the way I play depends on the team."

Like a number of other players from Holland, Van Hooijdonk has developed a reputation for being "difficult" or "arrogant". However, the Forest striker believes this reveals more about the different footballing cultures here and in his homeland than it does about the true nature of his personality. "I was never controversial in Holland," he claims. "In England, people are, maybe, not used to players answering back or coming up with their own opinions. Sometimes they take it personally, and I have to explain that I just want the best not just for me but them, too. I look for perfection. So I have seen things where I have had to say something – to have kept quiet would have been at odds with my mentality."

So is van Hooijdonk a misunderstood perfectionist or just a loudmouth big-head? The jury may still be out on that one, but Forest fans will care little about the final verdict as long as their record-signing continues to bang in the goals.

Patrick Vieira

ARSENAL

"English football... yes, I always like it and Arsenal is an international team."

Arsene Wenger liked the look of Patrick Vieira so much that he signed the young Frenchman to play for Arsenal before he had even become manager. Long-legged but hard as a rock, Vieira, frustrated after only nine first team appearances as cover for Marcel Desailly at Milan, was a snip at £3.5 million, and has looked every bit as good in his second season as he did in his first. Milan, in fact, have admitted they are kicking themselves for letting him go.

"He is a fighter," says Wenger of his capture. "Outside the field he has the look of being soft and casual, but on the field nothing frightens him. He reads the game well, he has quick feet, he's a good passer and a strong defender. Patrick has everything you need to play in England."

Sometimes, however, Vieira takes the "fighter" allusion a little too far: he has got a terrible disciplinary record and in March 1998 was involved in a huge final whistle rumpus at home to West Ham that saw him fined £12,000 by his manager for attacking John Moncur. But it is Vieira's fieriness and hardness in the tackle which make him such a priceless asset in the Gunners midfield. The Frenchman leaps at every free ball in midfield to set up priceless possession from balls that should, by rights, have gone to the hapless opposition.

What's more it's rare that such a hardman has the vision to play the ball to feet as devastatingly as Vieira can. There's graft to add to his craft. And he's no stranger to the scoresheet, often at crucial moments – his rasper in Arsenal's 3–2 win over Manchester United ended up a crucial strike that helped the Gunners immensely in their run-in to the final furlong of the Championship race.

In fact Vieira's such an asset to the club at such a young age that Wenger's been trying to tie him up to the club for life. "He could be a career player for Arsenal," says the Frenchman of his compatriot. The manager who signed Vieira before he arrived at the club doesn't want him to leave before he does.

Age
22

Date of Birth
23.6.76

Birthplace
Dakar, Senegal

Nickname:
What? (The only word of English he knew when he arrived at Highbury!)

Position
Midfielder

Goals & Games
Cannes 49 (2), AC Milan 2 (0)
Arsenal 64 (4)

Transfers
August 1996 – AC Milan to Arsenal (£3,5m)

Honours
Premier League, FA Cup 1998

THIS PAGE: CLASHING WITH GARY KELLY OF LEEDS ON 10 JANUARY, 1998

OPPOSITE PAGE: SCORING THE THIRD GOAL IN ARSENAL'S 3–1 WIN AGAINST NEWCASTLE ON 12 APRIL, 1998

Ian Walker

TOTTENHAM HOTSPUR

"Dad once said I was so laid back I was soft. I suppose I can give that impression, but I believe in trying to enjoy the game."

Age
26

Birth date
31.10.71

Birthplace
Watford

Nickname
None

Position
Goalkeeper

Games & Goals
Tottenham 192 (0), Oxford (loan) 2 (0)

Transfers
None. Signed professional forms from trainee in December 1989.

Honours
None

THIS PAGE: A TOP PREMIERSHIP KEEPER

OPPOSITE PAGE: LOOKING TO THE FUTURE DESPITE A POOR LAST SEASON

ast season was one to forget for Ian Walker. He spent the first half of it becoming something of a reluctant expert on goal nets, having ample opportunity to study the various Premiership styles on his frequent trips to retrieve the ball from the rigging.

It wasn't a question of Walker performing particularly badly, more that virtually every Saturday the Tottenham defence went on a Crocodile Dundee-style collective walkabout, leaving their floppy-haired keeper more exposed than a Chippendale at a hen party. The nadir came in a pre-Christmas non-performance against Chelsea at White Hart Lane, when the Spurs goalie was beaten five times in the second half as the West Londoners romped to a crushing 6–1 victory.

Surely it couldn't get any worse. But it did, as injury deprived Walker of his place in both the Tottenham line-up and the England squad in the build-up to the World Cup. It was a frustrating time for the Spurs shot-stopper, but at least he could talk about his worries with an understanding father – Mike, the Norwich manager and himself a former goalkeeper.

Despite his problems last season, there is no doubt that when he is fit (and playing behind a defence with fewer holes in it than the average slice of Swiss cheese) Walker junior is one of the Premiership's top keepers. Ray Clemence certainly thinks so. "He's got tremendous natural ability,' says England's goalkeeping coach.

"He's got an excellent pair of hands, reflexes and agility, but there are a couple of weaknesses he needs to work on."

Like most keepers, Walker is cagey about revealing precisely what those weak points are – fearing, perhaps, that opposition strikers might take advantage of them. He'll just be hoping that this season he won't have quite as many opportunities to brush up on his picking-the-ball-out-of-the-back-of-the-net technique which he got down to a fine art last time around.

Paolo Wanchope

DERBY COUNTY

"I have to keep my style, because if I change it, it's not Wanchope"

Age
22

Date of Birth
31.1.76

Birthplace
Costa Rica

Nickname
None

Position
Striker

Games & Goals
Derby County 30 (13)

Transfers
March 1997 – CS Herediano to Derby County (£600,000)

Honours
None

THIS PAGE: IN CELEBRATORY MOOD

OPPOSITE PAGE: SCORING FOR DERBY AGAINST ARSENAL ON 1 NOVEMBER 1997

all, long-limbed, beanpole-framed Paulo Wanchope looks as though he would be just as happy lining up alongside Michael Jordan as his Derby County teammates. Little wonder, then, that the 6ft 4in Costa Rican striker is a keen basketball player. Perhaps more surprising is that the gangly forward believes shooting baskets improves his penalty-box prowess. "Basketball is a big help because it teaches you how to get away from a guy and how to find and use room in a tight space," he explains. "I can also use my arms to hold off an opponent and turn."

Wanchope's unorthodox style has caused major headaches for Premiership defenders since he burst on the scene in March 1997, scoring a memorable individual goal on his debut at Old Trafford. Last season he continued to bamboozle opposition defences with his whacky repertoire of rubber-legged runs, ball-juggling dribbles and gawky all-knees-and-elbows aerial challenges. In the process Wanchope made a new high-profile fan in Alan Hansen – the "Match of the Day" pundit describing the Derby man's unusual play as a "nightmare for defenders".

How QPR must now wish they had not rejected the giant central American when he arrived at Loftus Road for a trial from Costa Rican club Herediano. The London club's loss was Derby's gain, however, as Rams manager Jim Smith decided to sign Wanchope after just one reserve match. The gamble certainly paid off as Wanchope gelled with the likes of Sturridge, Baiano and Eranio to form the Premiership's most exotic strikeforce – and one of its most potent.

Despite the goals and the adulation from the fans, Wanchope admits to feeling homesick for his native Costa Rica. "I miss the sun," he complains. "The weather here is so cold and I am still getting used to eating potatoes instead of rice."

Fortunately for Derby, Wanchope likes English defences a whole lot better than he likes our food.

Dennis Wise

CHELSEA

"When I get out on to that pitch there's only one thing I want to achieve and I'll do whatever it takes to achieve it."

Age
31

Date of Birth
16.11.66

Birthplace
Kensington

Nickname
The Rat

Position
Midfielder

Games & Goals
Wimbledon 135 (27), Chelsea 244 (46)

Transfers
July 1990 – Wimbledon to Chelsea (£1,6m)

Honours
FA Cup 1988 (Wimbledon)
FA Cup 1997, Coca-Cola Cup 1998
European Cup Winners' Cup 1998

THIS PAGE: TWO-FOOTED SKILL

OPPOSITE PAGE: WORKING WELL IN A TIGHT SPACE AGAINST LEICESTER

Dennis Wise had such a mixed campaign last year that it might have been scripted by the creator of Liquorice Allsorts. On the one hand, he was Chelsea's most consistent performer and captained The Blues to a Coca-Cola triumph against perennial Wembley-losers Middlesbrough. On the downside, he failed to reclaim a place in the England squad, and his tendency to collect yellow cards at the rate philatelists collect stamps meant he was suspended on three separate occasions.

Wise, though, has experienced more ups and downs than a hotel bell hop – so last season's highs and lows were par for the course. This, after all, is a man who has played in two FA Cup-winning teams but whose career almost ended before it began after he turned down the chance of a pro contract at Southampton when he became homesick. Fortunately, Wimbledon offered him a second chance and Wise – or "The Rat" as he was dubbed at Plough Lane – became a mainstay of the "Crazy Gang" side which stormed into the old First Division in 1986 and set about embarrassing the big boys.

Wise's part in The Dons' legendary 1988 FA Cup triumph over Liverpool meant a move to a more glamorous club was inevitable, and in 1990 the pocket-sized midfielder joined Chelsea in a deal which bolstered Wimbledon's meagre coffers by a cool £1.5 million. He ended his first season at The Bridge by scoring a freak goal with his backside on his England debut against Turkey.

Eleven more caps followed but his stop-start England career fizzled out when former Chelsea boss Glenn Hoddle took over at Lancaster Gate. Team-mate Steve Clarke finds this puzzling: "He's a much better player now than the Dennis Wise who was capped for England. He's gone from being a good club player, a little wide player getting crosses in, to someone who controls the whole game."

Last season Wise excelled in a new deep-lying midfield position where his aggressive tackling and thoughtful distribution launched numerous Chelsea attacks. "It's a different role for him," said then manager Ruud Gullit, before pointing out why he chose Wise to play there: "He's very skillful, two-footed, can pass with his left or right easily and he works well in small spaces." Working well in small spaces – that's Dennis, the chirpy cockney chimney sweep of Stamford Bridge.

Ian Wright

ARSENAL

"Dennis Bergkamp inspires me. I'm just pleased to be out there in the same team as him."

Age
34

Date of Birth
3.11.63

Birthplace
Woolwich

Nickname
Wrighty

Position
Striker

Games & Goals
Crystal Palace 225 (89)
Arsenal 221 (227)

Transfers
September 1991 – Crystal Palace to
Arsenal (£2,5m)

Honours
Coca-Cola Cup 1993, FA Cup 1993
Premier League, FA Cup 1998

Last season was a busy one for Ian Wright: he started a new career as a chat show host, appeared in more TV and magazine adverts than Rory McGrath, and became the official face of the Football Association during its campaign to win corporate sponsors. Oh, and he also found time to break Arsenal's individual goalscoring record and star in England's World Cup qualifying campaign.

Overall, though, it was a disappointing season for Wrighty. Injury prevented him from taking much part in the second half of Arsenal's Double-chasing campaign, while the emergence of young strikers Nicolas Anelka and Christopher Wreh appeared to threaten his long-term future at Highbury. Wright even managed to upset his own fans by shouting abuse and dropping his shorts at Arsenal supporters after the home defeat by Blackburn.

Nevertheless, Arsenal manager Arsene Wenger still sees Wright as a key member of his squad. "His hunger and enthusiasm stagger me," he says. "He is highly motivated to be a winner in all he does. He has lost half a yard of pace over 40 or 50 yards, yet what he still has is his electric pace over the first 10 yards. That beats defenders and helps score goals. In his thinking he wants 200 goals and then 210. That is the attitude of champions, the attitude of Ian Wright."

For his part, Wright believes his famously volatile temperament has mellowed, thanks to the influence of the professorial Frenchman. "I got frustrated with myself because I was always thinking that everything had to be perfect," he says, "but nothing is perfect. Arsene Wenger's made me realize how short my time in the game could be now. He's told me that I have to keep playing well to be in his teams. He's told me that I can play for as long as I want, but I have to reach his standards."

He may be approaching the twilight of his career, but few would bet against Wright meeting the Wenger standard this season as Arsenal aim to become champions of Europe.

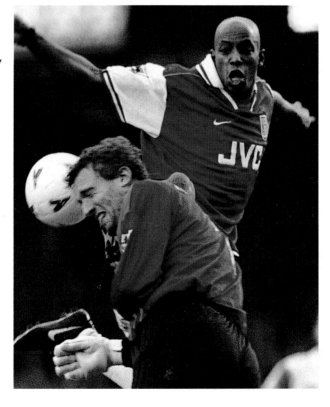

THIS PAGE: TOPPING BLACKBURN GOALKEEPER TIM FLOWERS ON 13 DECEMBER 1997

OPPOSITE PAGE: WRIGHTY IN FULL FLIGHT

Gianfranco Zola

CHELSEA

"I have always been content as I am. I have always felt quite big enough."

Age
31

Date of birth
5.7.66

Birthplace
Oliena, Sardinia

Nickname
Gorgon

Position
Striker

Games & Goals
Nuorese 31 (10), Torres 88 (21)
Napoli 105 (32), Parma 102 (49)
Chelsea 50 (16)

Transfers
Nuorese to Torres, Torres to Napoli
Napoli to Parma, Parma to Chelsea (£4.5m)

Honours
Italian Championship 1989/90 (Napoli)
Italian Cup 1992 (Parma)
European Cup Winners' Cup 1993 (Parma)
UEFA Cup 1995 (Parma)
FA Cup 1997 (Chelsea)
Coca Cola Cup 1998 (Chelsea)
European Cup Winners' Cup 1998

THIS PAGE: TONS OF SKILL IN SMALL BOOTS

OPPOSITE PAGE: TAKING A FLYING LEAP OVER FALLEN JOHN SCALES OF SPURS, 6 DECEMBER 1997

After taking the Premiership by storm in his first season – ending it with an FA Cup winners medal and the Footballer of the Year trophy – Chelsea's Gianfranco Zola struggled to reach the same dizzy heights last time around. But he still packed more skill in his size six boots than most of the players he shared a pitch with.

The tiny Sardinian's patchy form – at one point he went three months without a goal, the worst run of his career – was one of the mysteries of the season. One theory was that he was suffering from a loss of confidence after an ineffectual display against England in Rome which led to his being dropped from Italy's vital World Cup play-off against Russia. Another was that he was unsettled by then Chelsea boss Ruud Gullit's decision to break up his established partnership with Mark Hughes for a policy of rotating The Blues' star-studded forward line.

By the spring, though, the most famous Number 25 in Chelsea history began to again weave his own brand of special magic.

Zola was a key figure in Chelsea's Coca-Cola Cup semi-final destruction of Arsenal and, a few weeks later, was back to his dazzling best as The Blues surged past Real Betis and into the Cup Winners' Cup semi-finals.

This was the Zola who had become an instant favourite at Stamford Bridge with his brilliant close ball skills, perfectly-weighted passes and thunderous shooting.

Such qualities are also much appreciated by his teammates, as Mark Hughes makes clear. "He's so good on the ball it's untrue," says the Welsh international. "He sends in these inch-perfect passes which are so accurate that you don't have to break stride. If I cannot play well with a player like Zola than it's a bad reflection on myself."

The man who bought Zola to England, meanwhile, has no doubt about his greatest strength. "It's his technique," says Ruud Gullit. "Everyone says he makes it look so easy, but you have to look closely. He's small, of course, and that means he's capable of turning quickly, but it's so hard to do what he does." Hard, too, to stop Zola from doing his stuff – as any Premiership defender could tell you.

Predictions for the

O K, so you've met the stars of the show, but as everyone knows, one or two brilliant individuals don't make a team. You could put Dennis Bergkamp in the Doncaster Rovers line-up but it wouldn't guarantee the club a place in the Champions League. So what will happen to the teams in the Premiership next season? Can Manchester United reclaim the trophy that everyone was beginning to think belonged to them until Arsene Wenger came along? Can any of the teams that were promoted survive (they all went down last season)? Can Rob Jones ever score a goal for Liverpool? The answers to all these questions and more will be found over the coming months. But being an impatient lot, we've already worked out what we think will happen...

CHARLTON ATHLETIC

Charlton surprised just about everyone by taking the third Premiership place, beating Sunderland in the Wembley play-off. Alan Curbishley has created a neat, attractive team on a minuscule budget and – like Barnsley last year – the Addicks look set to become most fans' second-favourite team. Sadly, it's hard to see Charlton Athletic avoiding the popular Yorkshiremen's fate in 1998: a quick return to the Nationwide.

Prediction 20th (relegated)

WIMBLEDON

Ever since they made it into the top flight back in 1986 Wimbledon have been the pundits' tip for the drop, and every year the Crazies have made the critics eat humble pie. This, though, could be a season too far for The Dons. The warning signs were there last time around when Joe Kinnear's side finished as the Premiership's lowest scorers, with a paltry 34 goals. They'll need to improve on that total to have any chance of staying up, but are the funds available to buy that much-needed quality striker?

Prediction 19th (relegated)

Premier League

LEICESTER CITY

The Foxes finished a creditable 10th last season but only won six games at Filbert Street, fewer than Bolton or Barnsley – and look what happened to them! If that dodgy home form is repeated this time round, Leicester will struggle to hang on to their hard-won Premiership place. They could also do with more than 10 goals from last term's top scorer, the much-vaunted Emile Heskey.

Prediction 18th (relegated)

SHEFFIELD WEDNESDAY

Only Barnsley and Crystal Palace had a leakier defence last season than Sheffield Wednesday, and The Owls back line will require radical surgery if they are not to figure in the relegation frame once more. The saving grace for Wednesday is that in Di Canio and Carbone they have two proven matchwinners, and as long as the Italians stay free of injury the Hillsborough outfit should just manage to cling on to its Premiership status.

Prediction 17th

SOUTHAMPTON

Under-rated Southampton boss David Jones performed a minor miracle last season in guiding the South coast club away from the relegation rocks and into the calmer waters of mid-table. But will the Saints sink or swim this year? This is an ageing team – the likes of Palmer, Richardson, Hirst and, arguably, Le Tissier are well past their peak – and Jones may need to bolster his squad with some new, younger faces if he is going to keep his ship afloat.

Prediction 16th

OPPOSITE PAGE: CHARLTON'S CLIVE MENDONCA SLIDES HOME A SECOND GOAL AGAINST SUNDERLAND IN THE MATCH THAT TOOK THEM INTO THE PREMIER LEAGUE ON 25 MAY, 1998 AT WEMBLEY

THIS PAGE: DERBY'S FRANCESCO BAIANO GIVES VILLA'S EHIOGU A RUN FOR HIS MONEY ON 7 FEBRUARY, 1998

DERBY COUNTY

The Rams finished last season in a respectable 9th position but their form trailed away badly in the second half of the campaign. At first sight, Derby's problem is the old one of inconsistency but manager Jim Smith may be even more concerned about his team's tendency to fall to pieces once they concede (remember how Leicester helped themselves to four goals in the first 15 minutes at Pride park?) Fortunately, the likes of Wanchope, Baiano and Eranio will get enough goals at the other end to keep the East Midlanders out of trouble.

Prediction 15th

EVERTON

Everton only stayed up last term thanks to a last-day escape act that would have impressed Harry Houdini. Few tears would be shed outside Merseyside if Howard Kendall's unattractive team finally dropped into the Nationwide, but the likelihood is that The Toffees will enjoy a better campaign this season. Why? Well, they have money to spend, massive support and a batch of promising youngsters who lifted the FA Youth Cup in 1998. Who knows, they may even become exciting to watch.

Prediction 14th

MIDDLESBROUGH

Since Bryan Robson took over at the Riverside he's taken Boro' into the Premiership, back down to Division One and now into the Premiership once more. After all that excitement he'd probably settle for a quiet season of consolidation, and that's probably the best the Teesiders can hope for. Gazza, though, will make sure the season is never boring, and the likes of Merson, Branca and Armstrong will be worth watching too.

Prediction 13th

COVENTRY CITY

Having turned their relegation escape act into something approaching an art form, Coventry surprised many last season by finishing 11th – their highest league placing for nearly a decade. Much credit goes to manager Gordon Strachan and the fiery, fist-clenching Scot will expect even greater things from his team this year. The Sky Blues' big problem, though, is that they are too reliant on Dion Dublin and Darren Huckerby (the pair grabbed 32 of Coventry's 46 Premier League goals last term). Mid-table mediocrity awaits – unless they find at least one goalscoring midfielder.

Prediction 12th

THIS PAGE: TOTTENHAM'S SOL CAMPBELL CHASES THAT BALL

OPPOSITE PAGE: ROD WALLACE OF LEEDS SHOWS HIS GLEE AT A SCORE AGAINST NEWCASTLE LAST FEBRUARY

WEST HAM UNITED

Last season West Ham performed like world-beaters at Upton Park and dopes on their travels. Manager Harry Redknapp will be wracking his brain to work out why his side were so poor away from the East End, but he may never find the answer. Inconsistency has been The Hammers' middle name for years, and it's a tag they are unlikely to lose this season. It's a shame because the squad Redknapp has assembled should be good enough to figure in the UEFA Cup places.

Prediction 11th

TOTTENHAM HOTSPUR

Much-mocked from the day he arrived in north London brandishing a tube ticket, it's worth remembering that Christian Gross did the job Alan Sugar hired him to do last season: he saved Spurs from a potentially catastrophic drop into Division One. Mission accomplished, the iron-willed Swiss then instigated a massive clearout of White Hart Lane deadwood leaving his squad with a leaner, meaner look. Given a bit of good fortune with injuries, this could be a reasonable season for Spurs and their long-suffering fans.

Prediction 10th

NEWCASTLE UNITED

Surely it can't be as bad this time round! Second lowest scorers in the league, all their strikers injured or sold, the "Toongate" revelations – last season was a bit of a nightmare for Newcastle fans. True, there was a day out at Wembley in the Cup Final to enjoy, but even that ended in tears. This season will see an improvement, but Kenny Dalglish needs to perform major surgery on his squad if The Toon are to challenge for honours.

Prediction 9th

NOTTINGHAM FOREST

Promoted clubs in recent seasons have been living proof of the old adage "what goes up must come down". Forest, though, should buck that trend with something to spare. The Midlanders' main strength is in attack where the partnership between Kevin Campbell and Pierre van Hooijdonk is of top flight quality. Elsewhere there's a solid look about this Forest team, and in Dave Bassett they have a manager who knows the Premiership score.

Prediction 8th

BLACKBURN ROVERS

Roy Hodgson's first season in charge at Ewood Road tailed away disappointingly and although Blackburn grabbed a UEFA Cup place, they were unable to sustain a title challenge. Rovers are a well-organised, compact outfit spearheaded by a top striker in Chris Sutton, but unless they add a dash of much-needed flair to their graft they are unlikely to figure among the leading pack this season either.

Prediction 7th

ASTON VILLA

Relegation candidates in February, UEFA Cup qualifiers in May – aside from Arsenal, Aston Villa were the form team of the closing months of last season. Whether the Villans can maintain that sort of consistency over a whole campaign is another matter altogether, though. True, new boss John Gregory has made Villa extremely difficult to beat, but they may just be lacking a bit of craft to be considered title contenders.

Prediction 6th

LEEDS UNITED

After a miserable season in 1996/97 – when it was rumoured the club had changed its name to Leeds Nil – United were a different outfit last term, thanks largely to new faces like Jimmy Floyd Hasselbaink, Bruno Ribeiro and Alf Haaland. Make no mistake, George Graham will make Leeds a force in the land eventually, but his uncompromising defence and midfield may suffer more than most from the referees' clampdown on the tackle from behind.

Prediction 5th

LIVERPOOL

When will the Premiership title return to Meyseyside? It's now almost a decade since the championship pennant was last flown at Anfield and this, surely, will be Roy Evans' last crack at the title. With Robbie Fowler injured he will need to find a striker to support young paceman Michael Owen, but perhaps his greatest problems are in central defence – an area where The Reds have been vulnerable for some time. Frustratingly for the loyal Koppites, another season of under-achievement appears most likely.

Prediction 4th

CHELSEA

Two cups in his first three months in charge – Gianluca Vialli must be thinking this management game is child's play. Now, though, the challenge for the chrome dome Bridge boss is to turn The Blues from a cup team into one that can win the league. Fifteen defeats last season – only one fewer than relegated Bolton – suggests he has some to go, but there are too many outstanding players in this Chelsea squad for them not to be involved in the title race.

Prediction 3rd

MANCHESTER UNITED

Alex Ferguson will be livid that United ended up empty-handed last season after a campaign which promised so much. Injuries to key players exposed a lack of quality in depth in The Reds' squad last term, and that could be their Achilles heel this time, too. Yes, new signings like cultured defender Jaap Stam will make a difference, but United may just miss out on the title as Fergie chases his Holy Grail once more in the Champions' League.

Prediction 2nd

ARSENAL

Having won The Double, Arsenal could be forgiven for indulging in a spot of laurel-resting but Arsene Wenger will ensure his troops don't concede their title without a fight. This may be the last season The Gunners' fabled back five play together and they will be determined to go out at the top, while younger players like Nicholas Anelka and Patrick Viera can only improve. It won't be easy, but Arsenal have the resources and the desire to retain the championship and extend London's current monopoly of domestic silverware.

Prediction 1st

Predicted final table 1998-99

1	Arsenal	11	West Ham United
2	Manchester United	12	Coventry City
3	Chelsea	13	Middlesbrough
4	Liverpool	14	Everton
5	Leeds United	15	Derby County
6	Aston Villa	16	Southampton
7	Blackburn Rovers	17	Sheffield Wednesday
8	Nottingham Forest	18	Leicester City
9	Newcastle United	19	Wimbledon
10	Tottenham Hotspur	20	Charlton Athletic

TOP FORM: ARSENAL'S CHRISTOPHER WREH CELEBRATES A FIRST GOAL AGAINST BOLTON WANDERERS ON 31 MARCH, 1998

1997-98
Premier League Stats

Top Goalscorers
(Premier League only)

Dion Dublin	.18
Michael Owen	.18
Chris Sutton	.18
Dennis Bergkamp	.16
Kevin Gallacher	.16
Jimmy Floyd Hasselbaink	.16
Andy Cole	.15
John Hartson	.15
Paulo Wanchope	.13
Francesco Baiano	.12
Nathan Blake	.12
Paolo Di Canio	.12
Dwight Yorke	.12

The Ten Highest-scoring Teams

Manchester United	.73
Chelsea	.71
Arsenal	.68
Liverpool	.68
Leeds United	.57
Blackburn Rovers	.57
West Ham United	.56
Derby County	.52
Sheffield Wednesday	.52
Leicester City	.51

The Ten Leakiest Defences

Barnsley conceded	.82
Crystal Palace	.71
Sheffield Wednesday	.67
Bolton Wanderers	.61
West Ham United	.57
Everton	.56
Tottenham Hotspur	.56
Southampton	.55
Blackburn Rovers	.52
Derby County	.49

The Ten Teams Who Had the Most Shots

Liverpool (shots)	680
Manchester United	634
Arsenal	620
Chelsea	563
Blackburn Rovers	561
Tottenham Hotspur	561
Leeds United	549
Bolton Wanderers	524
Newcastle United	523
Aston Villa	519

The Ten Teams with a 100% Penalty Record

Chelsea	.6 out of 6
Coventry City	.6 out of 6
Derby County	.5 out of 5
Southampton	.5 out of 5
Barnsley	.4 out of 4
Leicester City	.4 out of 4
Bolton Wanderers	.3 out of 3
Sheffield Wednesday	.3 out of 3
Blackburn Rovers	.2 out of 2
West Ham United	.1 out of 1
Newcastle United	.1 out of 1

Five Players Sent Off More Than Once

David Batty (Newcastle United)	3 times
Slaven Bilic (Everton)	3 times
Paul Williams (Coventry City)	2 times
Stafan Eranio (Derby County)	2 times
John Hartson (West Ham United)	2 times

Yellow and Red Cards, plus Foul Chart

Team	Red cards	Yellow cards	Fouls
Leeds United	5 red cards	.84 yellow cards	.692 fouls
Everton	5 red	.84 yellow	.526 fouls
Barnsley	5 red	.70 yellow	.586 fouls
Coventry City	5 red	.70 yellow	.560 fouls
Bolton Wanderers	5 red	.68 yellow	.532 fouls
West Ham United	5 red	.60 yellow	.529 fouls
Blackburn Rovers	5 red	.55 yellow	.532 fouls
Sheffield Wednesday	4 red	.73 yellow	.524 fouls
Southampton	4 red	.61 yellow	.520 fouls
Crystal Palace	3 red	.71 yellow	.537 fouls
Chelsea	3 red	.64 yellow	.566 fouls
Newcastle United	3 red	.59 yellow	.518 fouls
Derby County	2 red	.81 yellow	.670 fouls
Arsenal	2 red	.68 yellow	.545 fouls
Tottenham Hotspur	2 red	.62 yellow	.492 fouls
Liverpool	2 red	.51 yellow	.464 fouls
Wimbledon	2 red	.45 yellow	.481 fouls
Leicester City	2 red	.43 yellow	.390 fouls
Aston Villa	2 red	.42 yellow	.461 fouls
Manchester United	1 red	.61 yellow	.472 fouls

The Ten "Snore Draw" Specialists

Wimbledon . . . . .8 (0-0 draws)
Coventry City 6
Everton 6
Blackburn Rovers 5
Bolton Wanderers 5
Newcastle United 5
Leicester City 4
Arsenal 4
Derby County 4
Leeds United 3

Barnsley were the only team who didn't have a single 0-0 draw last season.

Five Managers Who Didn't Last the Distance

Steve Coppell . . . . .(Crystal Palace)
Gerry Francis . . . . .(Tottenham Hotspur)
Ruud Gullit . . . . . .(Chelsea)
Brian Little . . . . . .(Aston Villa)
David Pleat . . . . . .(Sheffield Wednesday)

Seven Thrilling Draws

Bolton Wanderers 3–Derby County 3
Crystal Palace 3–West Ham United 3
Leeds United 3–Coventry City 3
Leicester City 3–Arsenal 3
Leicester City 3–Southampton 3
Newcastle United 3–Leicester City 3
Sheffield Wednesday–3 Liverpool 3
Tottenham Hotspur 3–Liverpool 3

The Six Biggest Thrashings of the Season

Manchester United 7–Barnsley 0
Blackburn Rovers7–Sheffield Wednesday 2
Barnsley 0–Chelsea 6
West Ham United 6–Barnsley 0
Tottenham Hotspur1–Chelsea 6
Manchester United–6 Sheffield Wednesday 1

The Clubs with the Most Home Wins

Arsenal 15
Chelsea 13
Liverpool 13
Manchester United 13
West Ham United 13

The Teams with the Most 1-0 Wins

Arsenal 7
Blackburn Rovers 6
Barnsley 5
Aston Villa 5
Leicester City 5
Newcastle United 5
Bolton Wanderers 4
Chelsea 4
Coventry City 4
Manchester United 4
Southampton 4
Wimbledon 4

The Teams with the Most Clean Sheets

Manchester United 20
Arsenal 19
Leicester City 15
Blackburn Rovers 14
Chelsea 14
Coventry City 13
Derby County 13
Liverpool 13
Wimbledon 13
Leeds United 11

And the Clubs with the Fewest Home Wins

Crystal Palace 2
Wimbledon 5
Leicester City 6
Barnsley 7
Bolton Wanderers 7
Everton 7
Tottenham Hotspur 7

The Five Strictest Referees

Gary Willard . .91 yellow cards .8 red cards
Graham Barber 87 yellow . . . . .10 red
Graham Poll . .83 yellow . . . . .7 red
Mike Reed . . .83 yellow . . . . .2 red
Uriah Rennie . .79 yellow . . . . .5 red

Five Naughty Boys

Alan Shearer – Appeared to kick Leicester's Neil Lennon in the face

Newcastle directors Douglas Hall and Freddie Fletcher – mocked The Toon Army and called Geordie women "dogs"

Leeds' team at Chelsea – two sent off and seven booked before half-time

Chris Sutton – turned down Glenn Hoddle's offer to play in England B team

Ian Wright – swore at Arsenal fans after home defeat by Blackburn

MICHAEL OWEN: THE LIVERPOOL LAD WAS ONE OF LAST SEASON'S TOP SCORERS IN THE PREMIER LEAGUE